To my dearest friend
Charlie
from
George F. Ghermanoff.
25 December 1936. *Hollywood, Calif.*

GOOD MEDICINE

WHEN I WAS A KID

GOOD MEDICINE

Memories of the Real West

CHARLES M. RUSSELL

With an Introduction by Will Rogers
and a Biographical Note by
Nancy C. Russell

GARDEN CITY PUBLISHING COMPANY, INC.
GARDEN CITY, NEW YORK

1194049

1194049

DEDICATION

"The West is dead!
  You may lose a sweetheart,
  But you won't forget her."—C.M.R.

THIS BOOK is lovingly dedicated to the West and to Charlie's friends. What a multitude, what a legion they were! Some of them were real saints in his eyes. And some of them were real sinners, too. And he knew it. And never cast a stone. But he would say, "My Brother, when you come to my lodge, the robe will be spread and the pipe lit for you."

NANCY C. RUSSELL.

CONTENTS

The people to whom the letters in this book were written,
with descriptive lines by Mrs. Russell

IX

INTRODUCTION

I AM awful glad that Mrs. Russell is allowing the Publishers to put out a Book like this. It's sorter like putting a name on a Tombstone: if you didn't, nobody but the family would ever know who was buried there. If it wasn't for a Book like this, Charlie Russell would just go down in history as an Artist, "The Great Cowboy Painter." We that knew him would all pass by his grave and know that there was more buried there than just a Painter. But the outside world wouldn't know it. They would be liable to figure him just "Another Artist." But he wasn't just "Another Artist." He wasn't "just another" anything. In nothing that he ever did was he "just another." I always felt that all that Painting gag was just a sort of a sideline with Charlie. I don't know that there is any grounds or foundation, but most of us come to think of an "Artist" of any line as a sort of half-breed Nut. We figure that if you took their "Art" away from 'em they would be pretty naked. In other words, every time we meet one of 'em in any line of Art he might be dealing in, we want to either hear him play his fiddle, or sing us a Song, or hand him his brush and tell him to start painting. But with old Charlie, if he had quit talking to you and started painting, you would-a got sore. It wasn't what you wanted. What you wanted was to hear him talk, or read what he said. He could paint you a Picture, and send you a letter with it, and you would value the letter more than you would the picture. Why,

13

Charlie didn't have a single earmark on him that we associate with the "Artist." Why he could *think* twice as straight as he could draw a line with a brush. He was a Philosopher. He was a great Humorist. He had a great underlying spiritual feeling, not the ordinary customs and habits that are supposed to mark, "What the well-dressed Christian is wearing this season," but a great sympathy and understanding for the man of the world, be he "Injun" or White. I don't know what religious outfit he sorter leaned to, if any of the present organized and chartered ones. But he sure had him one, and that was a belief in somebody or something, and that somebody or something was the one that he was going to leave to judge his fellow man,—he didn't believe that he was called on to do it himself. He was Cowboy enough to know that the final roundup ain't on this range, and you are not "parted" and classified by any other Humans. One Steer don't cut out another one and decide what market he will be shipped to. That's done by a man, or somebody of an entirely different race from cattle. And that's the way Charlie figured us. No other human ain't going to tell us where we are headed for. He would have been a Great Teacher,—I wanted to say Preacher, but I wouldn't a called him that because they feel called on to advise and regulate, and Charlie didn't. He believed in "Letting alone" and figuring it out for yourself, and when you got it figured out, it wasn't necessary to announce "how you had figured it out." He kinder figured that "Reforming" comes from a conscience, and not from advice. His belief was peace and contentment, let everybody go their own way, live their own lives, so long, of course, as it didn't trespass the rights of others. He wanted to see an "Injun" let alone. He believed that he was as happy, and as great a contribution to mankind, on a Pony as he is in a Ford. He believed that an "Injun"

14

living off the wild game of the Plains, and the fishes of the streams, and taking nothing from his fellow man, demanding no changes, might, if his example was followed, lead to a life of peace and contentment as beneficial as if you followed in the footsteps of a Wall Street broker. He had lived and associated with the Indians, and he knew that if you talked with a wise old Indian you would receive more real philosophy and knowledge than you could attending 32 Chamber of Commerce, Rotary, and Kiwanis Luncheons. He didn't believe that everything New was necessarily "Progress." He didn't think because we are going in Debt, that we are going ahead. He didn't think a "paved" street made a better Town. He knew that it only made a more comfortable town for an Automobilist to ride in. I doubt if he thought a round or two of Cocktails served to your Guests in your own home was any great improvement over going into the Silver Dollar and having a couple and not breaking any law.

He loved Nature,—everything he painted God had made. He didn't monkey away much time with the things that Man had made. He would rather paint a naked Indian than a fully clothed white man.

In people, he loved Human Nature. In stories, he loved Human interest. He ought to have been a Doctor. He wouldn't have had to use an Xray. He studied you from the inside out. Your outside never interested him. You never saw one of his paintings that you couldn't tell just what the Indian, the Horse and the Buffalo were thinking about.

If he had devoted the same time to writing that he had to his brush, he would have left a tremendous impression in that line. It's cropping out in every letter, in every line, his original observations, original ways of expressing them. He was a great story-teller. Bret Hart, Mark Twain or any of our old traditions couldn't paint a word picture with

15

the originality that Charlie could. He could take a short little yarn and make a production out of it. What a public entertainer he would have made. So few writers can tell their stuff. You are going to get a lot of it in these letters. Read between the lines. Don't just glance over the bare words. It's like his Pictures. He never painted a Picture that you couldn't look closely and find some little concealed humor in it. And that's the way with these,—every line has something more than appears on the bare paper.

It's hard for any man to tell what we did lose when we lost this fellow. No man, in my little experience, ever combined as many really unusual traits, and all based on One——Just Human. No conceit——You won't find a line or a spoken word ever uttered by him that would lead you to believe he had ever done anything that was the least bit out of the ordinary. You won't find a line of malice, hatred or envy (I haven't, as I write this, seen all the letters and contents of this book, but I just know it ain't there, for it wasn't in him). He had it in for Nobody.

I think every one of us that had the pleasure of knowing him is just a little better by having done so, and I hope everybody that reads some of his thoughts here will get a little aid in life's journey by seeing how it's possible to go through life living and let live. He not only left us great living Pictures of what our West was, but he left us an example of how to live in friendship with all mankind. A Real Downright, Honest to God, Human Being.

WILL ROGERS.

BIOGRAPHICAL NOTE

CHARLIE RUSSELL was what they call a good mixer. The gay times he was having in the big town interfered with his work, so in October, 1895, he decided to visit a friend in Cascade and fill some orders for pictures.

There was great excitement at the Roberts' home, where I lived, as a distinguished guest was expected. Charlie Russell, the cowboy artist, was coming for a visit. He knew a great deal about Indians, cowboys, and the Wild West. The Robertses had known him since he landed in Helena in 1880.

Just about supper-time, there was a jingle of spur-rowels on the back steps; then, Mr. Roberts brought his cowboy friend into the kitchen, where Mrs. Roberts and I were getting the supper on the table.

Charlie and I were introduced. The picture that is engraved on my memory of him is of a man a little above average height and weight, wearing a soft shirt, a Stetson hat on the back of his blonde head, tight trousers, held up by a "half-breed sash" that clung just above the hip bones, high-heeled riding boots on very small, arched feet. His face was Indian-like, square jaw and chin, large mouth, tightly closed firm lips, the under protruding slightly beyond the short upper, straight nose, high cheek bones, gray-blue deep-set eyes that seemed to see everything, but with an expression of honesty and understanding. He could not see wrong in anybody. He never believed any one did a bad act intentionally; it was always an accident. His hands were good-sized, perfectly shaped, with long, slender fingers. He loved jewelry and always wore three or four rings. They would not have been Charlie's hands any other way. Everyone noticed his hands, but it was not the rings that attracted, but the artistic, sensitive hands that had great strength and charm. When he talked, he used them a lot to emphasize what he was saying, much as an Indian would do.

Charlie was born in St. Louis, Missouri, on March 19th, 1864. As a small boy, he loved to hear about the pioneer life that had broken through and was supplanting the frontier with man-made civilization. He was interested in the stories of the fur and

Indian traders and the outfitting of boats that crawled up the Missouri River to Fort Benton, Montana. The levees of his home town had an irresistible fascination for the lad and he planned to run away and turn Indian fighter. School had no charm for him. He played hookey and the hours he should have been in school, he spent at the river front watching and talking with all sorts of men, unconsciously starting to build the foundation for his life work.

After several unsuccessful attempts to get West, he was sent to a military school at Burlington, New Jersey. He was made to walk guard for hours because book study was not in his mind. He would draw Indians, horses, or animals for any boy who would do his arithmetic in exchange. He loved American history, especially that of the country west of the Mississippi River. The teachers gave him up because he could not be made to study books—but pioneer life—yes, it was absorbed wherever he touched it, and made such an impression that it never left him.

When the military school failed to hold him or teach him application, he returned home. His father decided to try another way, so one day he said, "Would you like to go West, Charles? A gentleman I know is going to Montana and I was thinking of letting you go with him. You will stay but a few weeks, I imagine, until you will be glad to get back home and then go to work in school."

So, early in March, just before Charlie's sixteenth birthday, he started with Pike Miller by way of the Utah Northern Railroad and stage coach to Helena, Montana.

When they arrived there, the streets were lined with freight outfits. He saw bull teams, with their dusty whackers, swinging sixteen-foot lashes with rifle-like reports over seven or eight yoke teams; their string of talk profane and hide-blistering as their whips, but understood by every bull, mule-skinner, or jerk-line man. The jerk-line man would be astride the saddled nigh-wheeler, jerking the line that led to the little span of leaders. These teams were sometimes horses and sometimes mules, and twelve to fourteen span to a team, often pulling three wagons chained together, all handled by one line.

It was also ration-time for the Indians in that section, so the red men were standing or riding in that quiet way of theirs, all wearing skin leggings and robes. They did not have civilized clothes. The picturesqueness of it all filled the heart and soul of this youthful traveler and he knew that he had found his country, the place he would make his home; but he did not know what a great part he was to take in recording its history for the coming generations.

18

In Helena, Mr. Miller outfitted, buying a wagon and four horses, two of them being Charlie's. With their load of grub, they pulled for the Judith Basin country, where Miller had a sheep ranch. The wagon trails were very dim and rough and they had a hard time crossing the Crazy Mountains, as one of their horses played out. But they did arrive—a very weary outfit. Charlie said that that trip settled it with him so far as driving a team and wagon was concerned. Thereafter, pack and saddle horses were his favorite way of traveling and he never changed. He often said to me, "You can have a car, but I'll stick to the hoss; we understan' each other better."

He did not stay with Miller but a few weeks, as the sheep and Charlie did not get along at all well. When they split up, Charlie didn't think Miller missed him much, as he was considered pretty "ornery."

He took his two horses and went to a stage station where he had heard they needed a stock-herder, but word of his dislike for the sheep job had gotten there ahead of him and they were not willing to trust their horses with him, so he did not get the job.

Leading his pack horse and carrying a very light bed, Charlie pulled out for the Judith River, where he made camp and picketed his horses. He had a lot of thinking to do. As he unrolled and started to make his bed, a man's voice from out of the shadows said, "Hello, Kid! What are you doing here?"

Half scared, he turned to find a stranger sizing him up.

"Camping," he answered.

"Where's your grub?" the stranger inquired.

"Haven't any."

"Where you going?"

"To find a job."

"Where you from?"

On being told, he said, "You better come over and camp with me; I got a lot of elk meat, beans and coffee. That ought to feel pretty good to the inside of a kid like you."

So Charlie threw in with him. The man was Jake Hoover, hunter and trapper, and a lifelong friend to the boy he met there on the trail. Hoover's manner of life suited young Russell, who longed for the open country and its native people.

Jake advised him to get rid of his horses, as they were big team horses and one a mare. Jake said this country was no place for a lady-horse; if she took a notion, she would leave and take every other horse with her.

In a few days, he met a bunch of Piegan Indians and traded for two smaller horses, one a pinto, that he named "Monte." They were kids together and, when Monte died in 1904, Charlie had ridden and packed him thousands of miles. They were always together and people who knew one, knew the other. They didn't exactly talk, but they sure savied each other.

Charlie lived with Jake about two years. They had six horses; a saddle horse apiece and pack animals. They hunted and trapped, selling bear, deer and elk meat to the settlers, and sending the furs and pelts which they got in to Fort Benton to trade.

In the Spring of 1881, Charlie's father sent him money to come home. To acknowledge it, Charlie wrote a letter in which he said, "Thanks for the money, which I am returning. I can't use it, but some day I will make enough; then I will come home to see you folks."

By the Spring of 1882, he had saved enough to return to St. Louis, where he stayed about four weeks. He could not resist the call to Montana, so he came back with a cousin, Jim Fulkerson, who died of mountain fever at Billings two weeks after they arrived.

Again alone, with four bits in his pocket and 200 miles between him and Hoover, things looked mighty rocky. He struck a fellow he knew and borrowed a horse and saddle from him until he could get to his own; then, started for the Judith Basin country.

There was still a little snow, as it was early in April, but after riding about fifteen miles, he struck a cow outfit, coming in to receive a thousand dogies for the Twelve Z and V outfit up in the Basin. The boss, John Cabler, hired him to night-wrangle horses. They were about a month on the trail and turned loose at Ross Fork, where they were met by the Judith roundup.

Charlie was getting back to Hoover and the country he knew, but he'd had a taste of the cow business and wanted more. The Judith roundup foreman had just fired his night-herder and Cabler gave him a good recommend, so he took the herd. Charlie said it was a lucky thing no one knew him, or he never would have gotten the job.

When old man True asked who he was, Ed Older said, "I think it's 'Kid' Russell."

"Who's Kid Russell?"

"Why," said Ed, "it's the Kid that drew S. S. Hobson's ranch so real."

"Well," says True, "if that's 'Buckskin Kid,' I'm bettin' we'll be afoot in the morning."

So you see the kind of a reputation he had. He was spoken of as "that ornery Kid Russell," but not among cow men. He held their bunch and at that time they had about four hundred saddle horses. That same Fall, old man True hired him to night-herd beef and for the most part of eleven years, as he says, he sang to their horses and cattle.

In the Winter of 1886, there was a bunch wintering at the O H Ranch. They had pretty nice weather till Christmas. When the snow came, there was two feet on the level. The stage line had to have men stick willows in the snow so they would know where the road was. Those willows, on parts of the road, were standing in May.

There was good grass in the Fall. The country was all open—no fences. The horses went through the Winter, fat, since they could paw, breaking the snow's crust and getting through to grass. A cow won't; they are not rustlers. They would go in the brush, hump up and die; so the wolves fattened on the cattle.

Charlie was living at the ranch. There were several men there and among them was Jesse Phillips, the owner of the O H. One night, Jesse had a letter from Louie Kaufman, one of the biggest cattlemen in the country, who lived in Helena. Louie wanted to know how the cattle were doing. Jesse said, "I must write a letter and tell Louie how tough it is." Charlie was sitting at the table with Jesse and said, "I'll make a sketch to go with it." So he made a little watercolor about the size of a postcard and said to Jesse, "Put that in your letter."

Jesse looked at it and said, "Hell, Louie don't need a letter; that will be enough."

The cow in the picture was a Bar R cow, one of Kaufman's brand. On the picture Charlie wrote, "Waiting for a Chinook and nothing else."

That little watercolor drawing made Charlie famous among stockmen and was the wedge which opened up the field of history in this part of the West for him. He still did not know he was about to graduate from this School of Nature, to take up his life work.

In 1888, he went to the then Northwest Territory and stayed about six months with the Blood Indians. They are one branch of the Blackfeet tribes. He became a great friend of a young Indian, named "Sleeping Thunder." Through their friendship, the older men of the tribe grew to know Charlie and wanted him to marry one of their women and become one of them. The Red Men of our Northwest love and think of Charlie as a kind of medicine man because he could draw them and their life so well.

He learned to speak Piegan a little but could use the sign language well enough to get along anywhere with any tribe of the plains that he ever met, as the sign talk is universal among the American Plains Indians. Whether with white man or red, with a lump of wax or a few tubes of paint, he drew, painted and modelled, all his spare time, just for the satisfaction of recording what he saw and to entertain his friends. Still, he did not dream of the great work ahead of him.

In the Spring of 1889, he went back to Judith to his old job of wrangling. The captain was Horace Brewster, the same man who had hired him in 1882, on Ross Fork. All these years there had been the mixing with, studying the habits of, and drawing all the different types of men and animal life.

Living with a trapper, he got close to the hearts of the wild animals. He saw them in their own country; got to know their habits. Knew them with their young and saw their struggle against their enemies, especially Man.

But the West was changing. Stage coaches and steamboats carried the white people west, while the freighters with bull, mule and horse teams, played their great part in bringing what we call civilization to this Northwest country.

Charlie was here to see the change. He did not like the new; so started to record the old in ink, paint and clay. He liked the old ways best. He was a child of the West before wire or rail spanned it; now, civilization choked him. Even in 1889, when the Judith country was becoming well settled and the sheep had the range, he resented the change and followed the cattle north to the Milk River, trying to stay in an open range country.

In the Fall of 1891, he received a letter from Charlie Green, a gambler, better known as "Pretty Charlie," who was in Great Falls, saying that if he would come to that camp, he could make $75.00 a month and grub. It looked good, so Charlie saddled his gray, packed Monte, the pinto, and took the trail. When he arrived, Green introduced him to Mr. K., who pulled out a contract as long as a stake rope, for him to sign.

Everything he modelled or painted for one year was to be Mr. K.'s. Charlie balked. Then K. wanted him to paint from early morning until six at night, but Charlie argued there was some difference in painting and sawing wood. So they split up and Charlie went to work for himself. He joined a bunch of cowpunchers, a round-up cook and a prizefighter out of work. They rented a shack on the south side. The feed was very short at times but they wintered.

Next Spring, he went back to Milk River and once more lived the range life. But it had changed. That Autumn, he returned to Great Falls, took up the paint brush and never rode the range again.

We met in October, 1895, and were married in September, 1896. With $75.00, we furnished a one room shack there in Cascade, where we lived one year. There was little chance to get orders for pictures in such a small town, so we moved to Great Falls, where Charlie could meet a few travelers and get an occasional order.

Charles Schatzlein, of Butte, Montana, was one good friend. He had an art store, and gave Charlie a good many orders, making it possible for us to pay our house rent and feed, but, as Charlie said, "The grass wasn't so good."

One time, Mr. Schatzlein came to visit us.

"Do you know, Russell," he said, "you don't ask enough for your pictures. That last bunch you sent me, I sold one for enough to pay for six. I am paying you your price, but it's not enough. I think your wife should take hold of that end of the game and help you out."

From that time, the prices of Charlie's work began to advance until it was possible to live a little more comfortably.

In 1900, Charlie got a small legacy from his mother, which was the nest egg that started the home we live in. After the cottage home was finished and furnished, Charlie said, "I want a log studio some day, just a cabin like I used to live in."

That year, 1903, the studio was built on the lot adjoining the house. Charlie did not like the mess of building so he took no more than a mild interest in the preparations. Then, one day, a neighbor said, "What are you doing at your place, Russell, building a corral?"

That settled it. Charlie just thought the neighbors didn't want the cabin mixed in with the civilized dwellings and felt sure they would get up a petition to prevent our building anything so unsightly as a log house in their midst. But way down in his heart, he wanted that studio. It was the right kind of a work-shop for him, but he was worried at what he thought the neighbors would say, so said he would have nothing to do with it.

He made no further comment, nor did he go near it until one evening, Mr. Trigg, one of our dearest friends, came over and said, "Say, son, let's go see the new studio. That big stone fireplace looks good to me from the outside. Show me what it's like from the inside."

Charlie looked at me kind of queer. The supper dishes had to be washed. That was my job just then, so Charlie took Mr. Trigg out to see his new studio that he had not been in. When they came back into the house, the dishes were all put away.

Charlie was saying, "That's going to be a good shack for me. The bunch can come visit, talk and smoke, while I paint."

From that day to the end of his life he loved that telephone pole building more than any other place on earth and never finished a painting anywhere else. The walls were hung with all kinds of things given him by Indian friends, and his horse jewelry, as he called it, that had been accumulated on the range, was as precious to him as a girl's jewel box to her.

One of Charlie's great joys was to give suppers cooked over the fire, using a Dutch oven and frying pan, doing all the cooking himself. The invited guests were not to come near until the food was ready. There was usually bachelor bread, boiled beans, fried bacon, or if it was Fall, maybe deer meat, and coffee; the dessert must be dried apples. A flour sack was tucked in his sash for an apron and, as he worked, the great beads of perspiration would gather and roll down his face and neck.

When it was ready, with a big smile, he would step to the door with the gladdest call the oldtime roundup cook could give—"Come and get it!"

There was a joyous light in his eyes when anyone said the bread was good, or asked for a second helping of anything. When no more could be eaten, he would say, "Sure you got enough; lots of grub here."

Then the coffee pot would be pushed to one side, frying pan and Dutch oven pulled away from the fire, and Charlie would get the "makins." Sitting on his heels among us, he would roll a cigarette with those long, slender fingers, light it, and in the smoke, drift back in his talk to times when there were very few, if any, white women in Montana. It was Nature's country. If that cabin could only tell what those log walls have heard!

The world knows about his paintings and modelling, but his illustrated letters are novel because of his spelling and lack of book learning. The perfection of his humor is not of books, but comes direct from the life in the West that he lived and loved.

The State University of Montana is not prodigal in giving honors, but Charlie justified himself as the greatest student and teacher of the West in his time and so won the fourth honorary degree of Doctor of Laws ever given by that University. Charlie said, "Nature has been my teacher; I'll leave it to you whether she was a good one or not."

It will be next to impossible in a few years for anyone to recall what he said, so this book is gotten together that the many may know Charlie and his philosophy through his letters, as do the few who have received them. To those who have been kind enough to loan their letters for this purpose, I express my sincere thanks and appreciation. I am sure they will be glad to have participated in this effort to leave as a permanent record this memorial of the love of a great man for a big country and its people.

NANCY C. RUSSELL.

Publisher's Note: In the general make-up of this book the publishers have constantly kept before them the desirability of reproducing the letters of Charles M. Russell, both pictures and text, as nearly as possible in the identical manner in which they were written. Mr. Russell's own spelling, punctuation, and spacing have been followed in cases where the letters have been reproduced in type. To have prettified his text for typographical reasons would have destroyed much of the charm of the book and much of its historical authenticity. As nearly as possible the reproduction gives us the man and the artist who was so well loved by people who know and understand the old West.

In order to give a wide selection of letters and as many of the illustrations as possible, it has been necessary to delete lines or paragraphs from the letters here and there. This has been a matter of keen regret to the publishers. All deletions are indicated by ellipses.

The letters are not published in chronological order for reasons connected with the technical reproduction. As a whole the effort has been to give a pleasing relationship between color and text. Where the date of the letter appears on the picture it is not repeated in the printed text, but wherever a date appeared on the original letter it is reproduced in one place or the other. Some of the letters were not dated at all and consequently bear no dates in the book.

The only places where Mr. Russell's original spelling has not been carried out are a few instances of obvious slips of the pen where the intention of the writer would be obscured by a too faithful reproduction of the letter. Typographical consistency has been sacrificed wherever by so doing a clearer picture of Charlie Russell could shine through these pages to the reader.

WHERE TRACKS SPELL WAR OR MEAT

Nature taught her child
   To read, to write and spell,
And with her books before him
   He reads his lesson well.

Each day is but a page
   His God, the sun, has turned.
Each year, a chapter nature taught
   Her child has read and learned.

A broken twig, a stone is turned
   Disturbed by passing feet
His savage eye has caught it all
   For tracks spell war or meat.

Nature holds his Bible
   With pages open wide,
He questions not her miracles
   'Tis done; he's satisfied.

He loves his mother country
   Where all her creatures trod,
Yet he is called a heathen
   Who has always lived with God.

Courtesy of Dr. Philip G. Cole. This poem was written by Mr. Russell to go with the picture of the same title, which is here reproduced as a lining paper.

Friend Bill

I am sending you the long promised sketch   it represents an old time cow dog mounted on a bronk

In this day of fancy roaping the trick hes turning aint so much. but I remember when a hand that could do this from the top of a stiff necked bronk was not classed with punkin rollers

My wife got a letter from your best half asking us to come and camp with you all   we both thank you verry much but we wont worke your range this year   wev got a six months old boy at our camp and we think hes a little young for trail work so we are going to class herd him a while   The Stork dident bring him   he had been on earth about three moons when he was thrown in my cut but hes waring my Iron now and I hope nobody ever vents it

now Bill if you ore your folks ever drift this way dont forgit my camp   theres grub and blankets for you and yors aney time   with best whishes to you all from us both

your friend

C M Russell

Friend Joe

I have received sevral letters from you so I will answer the last one   Mame told about the talk she had with you over the fone but long range talks are like letters not like the real thing

Im sorry to here that old man Cross is sick and hope by this time hes all right.

I got a letter from Krieg a long time ago, but have not answered it yet   Im mighty slow coming across with letters but it aint becaus I dont think of my Friends you know that Joe

We went to Arizona since I saw you on a trip with the Eaton party   I saw a fiew folks like the above sketch   It is a great country wild and makes good picture stuff. the Indians are not as good as there northern brothers eather in looks ore dress but a bunch of Navajoes mounted in there country of red sand makes a good picture and for a man who likes mountians and Indians I know no better country

I was up to see Frank Linderman last fall   he has built a big cabon on Flat Head lake and is living there with his family   Its about fifteen miles above Summers it is a bautiful place   when I was there the cabon was not finished so frank and I camped in a loge and we shure had a good time.

Now joe if the three Scheuerleys do come west dont forget our camp   the lach strings out   Percy Rabon was just here and sends his regards   I wish you could see our boy jack   hes 17 months old   he runs all over the place now and it keeps both of us buisy hearding him   he has a language of his own that we don't savy.

This is a long letter for me so I guess Il close with best whishes from Nancy and I to the three of you

Your Friend
C M Russell

Miss Josephine and Mrs Trigg send regards

C. M. RUSSELL
GREAT FALLS, MONTANA

Friend Sweet

I am returning the tin tipe an I guess you think its about time. I had a good copy made of it which I will al ways keep   it shure brings back the old days an that trip to White Sulpher over the south fork trail

If I rember right I was gide but failed an lost the blaze   you run out of Climax an was forsed to chew Durham but we made up for lost time when we reached the Burg

with best whishes to your self and Wife an all old timers

Your friend
C M Russell

Dear Mr. Hart

I received som newspaper pictures which reminded me of the photographes and letter you sente me som months ago. I liked them very much. I guess you think I'm a long time saying so but you wont have to go far in this letter to find out that writing is no pass time with me its

WORK   I am average on talk but hand me thes. tools

an I'm deaf an dum you said in your letter you hoped I enjoyed Your play I certainly did

I have your photo hanging in my little parler an old cow puncher friend droped in the other day an was laking at the pictures an when he run on to your photo he asked

whos the Sky Pilot

well if you ever drift west again which I hope you will an sight the smoke

of my camp

Come and as our red brothers say my pipe will be lit for you

June 29
1902

Yours Sincerly

CM Russell

The Manhatten has sent for the Pigan it
is good
the Antilopes hart would be glad to smoke with maney
tribes   at the big canpe
but for three moons the trails have hidden beneath
the snow
an it is not good to travel far when the poney
wares his hair long

My arme is short an cannot reach the pipe
you light for me
but our harts are together- and the same
it is good
              Antilope

32

Friend Ted   May 13 1919

I got the picture and letter both the 9th and you and your old hoss will deck the walls of my shack always   and when ever I look at the picture my memory will drift back over trails long since plowed under by the nester to days when a pair of horse ranglers sat in the shaddoes of thair horses and wached the grasing bunches of cyuses   these cyuses had all heard the fiddle mouth harp and the maney songs sung by thair riders   even the war drum of the red men was no novelty to them   but the day I speak of it was different   every hoss with head up and ears straightened listened for one of the ranglers was a musician . . .

I remember one day we were looking at buffalo carcus and you said Russ I wish I was a Sioux Injun a hundred years ago   and I said me to Ted thairs a pair of us

I have often made that wish since an if the buffalo would come back tomorrow I wouldent be slow shedding to a brich clout and youd trade that three duce ranch for a buffalo hoss and a pair ear rings   like many I know, your all Injun under the hide and its a sinch you wouldent get home sick in a skin lodge

Old Ma Nature was kind to her red children and the old time cow puncher was her adopted son . . .

Your friend
C M Russell

33

C. M. RUSSELL
GREAT FALLS, MONTANA

Friend Theo

March 19 1920

Friend Theo

Im down here in what is called by some the worlds pick nick ground and I think thats a good name caus theyv shure picked a nick in my bank role

Early history says this country was the home range of the hold up till the law makers came and hung up a bounty for the head ore scalp of all gents of the road when they opened the law on road agents and put on a bounty everybody quit mining and went hunting and for many years Califonia was smoky and in actions resembled Bill Harts pictures   the Digger Injun lived in caves and fed on roots and acorns this vegitaron grazing made him non war like and pease loving so they dident take sides in aney of the killings   Spaniard Mexicon ore Yankee all looked alike and was much easier to get along with after they quit breathing so they just sat at the mouth of thair caves and wached thair gold loving brothers exturmanate one an other The hold ups were in the megority so at the cleanup there wasent enough reformers left to start aneything so the Diggers lived in safety for quite a while   all this happened long ago   the Bandits who wached the roads like the Digger have gon   But history repeats   the Digger has not returned but the hold up is here   his work is not as corse as it was   In days gon by he had a good horse under him and went heeled to the teeth   if he lived long it was because his guns were faster and shurer than those

of the law   his home was aney where he unsaddled his horse   this kind only lives in history but right now maby its his ofspring   thair lives in Califonia a hold up man that makes his Great Grand Dad look like a watermelon theif   This gent rides a Pierce Arrow ore some other wagon that causts more than 500 head of the mistang breed his Great Grand Dad rode   This new hold up dont have to sit up nights and wach the roads and trails   he owns a hotel a restraunt or a bunch of bungiloos   in these he traps and skins the tourist. To steal is to take when thairs no one looking of corse the Califonian dont do that he stands in front of you when he takes your role and thairs no law agin it. but law has changed   in early days they hung ore shot his Great Grand Dad for the same kind of worke

   Theo if you ore aney of your friends ever come down to this Pick nick, bring one of them roles with a rubber band on it the kind that would choke a cow   Stay a month and Im betting you wont need a rubber   right now what I got left wouldent choak a chick a dee

   with best whishes to you and yours

Your friend
C M Russell

866 Chester av north
Pasidana
Califonia

Miss Josephine Dear Friend

This is a portrait
of Bills Grate Grate
Grate Gran Dad
by Renbrandt
you will now
under stand why
Bill has turned
that hair loos
he hopes some
day to look like
Grand pa
below you well
see the famely
Coat. of. armes
It is hard for a white 
man to interpret think
but I would, it means
to gether we are strong
though the sausage is
no stronger than its weakest
link it still hangs together
an you know how strong Duch
chees is
the strin I think de notes joy

Your friend
C M Russell
Sept 22
1912

Smell Smell
Smell
Smell

Cheese
Smell ant

Soul ant

Sausage rampant

36

Nove 26
1925

Ralf Budd

Dear Mr. Budd

this is Thanksgiving day an Im thanking you for the good time you gave us last summer

turkey is the emblem of this day and it should be in the east but the west owes nothing to that bird but it owes much to the humped backed beef in the sketch above

the Rocky mountians would have been hard to reach with out him

he fed the explorer   the great fur trade wagon tranes felt safe when they reached his range

he fed the men that layed the first ties across this great west   Thair is no day set aside where he is an emblem

the nickle weares his picture dam small money for so much meat   he was one of natures bigest gift and this country owes him thanks

the picture you sent a photo of that I painted was made a long time ago   It was made to reprsent Fater DeSmit on the Missouri River

hoping you and yours are all well   I am

your friend

C. M. Russell

Mrs. R——sends best regards

Here's to all old timers, Bob,
  They weren't all square it's true,
Some cashed in with their boots on—
  Good old friends I knew.

Here's to the first ones here, Bob,
  Men who broke the trail
For the tenderfoot and booster
  Who come to the country by rail.

Here's to the man with the gold pan
  Whose heart wasn't hard to find,
It was big as the country he lived in,
  And good as the metal he mined.

Here's to the rustler that packed a notched gun
  And didn't call killins' sins,
If you'd count the cows and calves in his herd
  You'd swear all his bulls had twins.

Here's to the skinner with a jerk line
  Who could make a black snake talk,
An' could string his team up a mountain road
  That would bother a human to walk.

Here's to the crooked gambler
  Who dealt from a box that was brace,
Would pull from the bottom in stud hoss
  An' double cross friends in a race.

Here's to the driver that sat on the coach
  With six reins and the silk in his grip,
Who'd bet he could throw all the ribbons away
  An' herd his bronk team with his whip.

Here's to the holdup an' hoss thief
  That loved stage roads an' hosses too well,
Who asked the stranglers to hurry
  Or he'd be late to breakfast in Hell.

Here's to the 'whaker that swung a long lash
An' his bulls bawled with fear when he spoke,
He'd swear on a hill he wouldn't drop trail
If every bull starved in the yoke.

So here's to my old time friends, Bob,
I drink to them one and all,
I've known the roughest of them, Bob,
But none that I knew were small.
Here's to Hell with the booster,
The land is no longer free,
The worst old timer I ever knew
Looks dam good to me.

Sentiments
of your friend
CMRussell
1911

Friend Bill:[1]

I received your letter; allso headdress and Mame got the spoon and we both send thanks.

We all had a good Christmas; got lots of gifts and we would have enjoyed having you here. You were so long coming a cross with your answer that I begin to think you had crossed the big creek an throwed in with your Duch relations agin them frog and beef eaters. That namesake of yours is sure a ware like proposition.

Young Boy and Little Bear were here the other day and wanted to know all about the ware. Little Bear seemed quite pleeased to hear that boath sides were whites and when I said that there had been over a million killed, a broad smile covered his kindly face. No doubt, he would have liked to have been thair at the hair gathering; especuly, the English killed. Thair's nothing he likes about an Englishman but his hair. In old days, his Gran Dad used it to trim leggins with it and what was good enough for that old man looks good to his grand son and I don't doubt but that Little Bear has some of these souvaniers hid away that he gathered douring the Real War in Canada. . . .

Your friend
C. M. Russell

[1]Letter not dated. Written during the Great War.

Feb 8th
1923

Richard Jones
Friend Dick

    You will see by the sketch I am among the palms and flowers but Im still packing coal   sun shine in this country is like near beer   it looks good thats all   in most countrys flowers and palm trees mean warmth but that dont go here   Aney thing that grows here would thrive aney where in Glacier Park

    tell Bull Trout thairs lots of fishing here from shark to smelt   the ocion aint fifty yards from my door   Frank Linderman and me are going clam fishing in a fiew days   Frank lives next door   we get these with a shovel and working around a furnis so many years Im shure handy with that tool   When they fish with a shovel its a sinch Il bring back the goods   Dick I would like to step in to the Como right now   give my regards to the bunch including the young lady

    best whishes to you and yours

Your friend

If you have time tell me the news.

C M Russell

Address 509 East Cabrillo Boulevard Santa barbara

C. M. RUSSELL

GREAT FALLS, MONTANA

March 22, 1923

To my Friend Ed Borein

If hosses were health I'd comb the range
and trim every band I knew
You'd go to the end of a long long trail
with a top hoss under you

C M Russell

41

Oct 13
1912
Great Falls
Mont

Friend Guy

I received your postal and letter an was glad to here from you

You were so bussy when I left I did not get to thank you for the good time we had at the Stampede

I came west 31 years ago   at that time baring the Indians an a fiew scaterd whites the country belonged to God   but now the real estate man an nester have got moste of it grass side down an most of the cows that are left feed on shuger beet pulp but thank God I was here first an in my time Iv seen som roping an riding but never before have I seen so much of it bunched as I did at Calgary   Ive seen som good wild west showes but I wouldent call what you pulled off a show. it was the real thing an a whole lot of it

those horses judging from the way they unloded them twisters wasent broke for grandmas pheaton, they were shure snakey an your cattel dident act like dary stock

to me   I dont think aney I saw had been handled by milk maids   they were shure a supprise to those old cow poneys that had been running short horns all there life. It wasent hardly fair to spring a gray hound waring hornes an Guy football ain't so gentel—the bull ring an prise fighting is som rough but bull doging those long horns makes all other dangerous sports look like nursery games

I am not alone in my praise of the Stampede   there are other men better judges than myself make the same talk.

With best whishes from
my wife and I
to you and yours

your friend
C M Russell

May 20 1925

Dick Bodkin
Friend Dick

judging from the way you stick in the oringe belt your warped on that country. Since you started riding for cameras your harder to locate than Kid Kurry. Jack gave me your address.

Dick I used to make fun of moove cow Boys but since I saw them worke my hats off once an old Injun told me that it wasent the head that made men brave it was the hart if his talk was right these moove punchers has inlargment of the hart and shrinking of the head   I seen them ride down hills that I wouldent do with a ladder   Im an old man now but I still like to ride a frendly horse but I dont want no moove director to pick trails for me. I know a fiew moove men down on the screen range   Tom Mix Bill Rogers Bill Hart Neal Hart Buck Conner Harry Carey   I knew Tom Mix when he owned a saddle and a pair of spurs and if youd asked him where Holly wood was he wouldent have known if it was a line camp ore a state but Mix is a regular man and Im glad he got the coin   all the men I know down thair are good men and worth beeing friendly with   aney of them you meet give my regards to. things are about the same around here   I see your brother Jack every day   Saw your Mother and she wants you to come home and make her a visit   She looked well   you ought to come home onc and a while and see your folks   the country looks better than it hase for a long time good grass.   woldent you like to get a horse under you and ride over som real grass country and get down on your belly and drink from a cold mounion stream

with best whishes to you and yours   Your friend

Hows the little girl   C M Russell

44

Will James   May 30 1924
Friend James

I got your letter and sketch and was glad to here from you   you asked how I would handel such an animal   If I ever saw it I wouldent get close unough to handle Iv known cow punchers that saw such things after hanging around a rode ranch ore burg but non of them tuck a rope down but they used a quirt mighty nasty and as I am better with a quirt than a rope Id use the one I know best

I have been getting your stuff in Scribners   its good both pictures and writing.

. . . I have been in bade shape for nearly a year but am better now   tryed to get on a horse the other day at Harry Carys ranch but couldent mak it   cant ride nothing wilder than a wheel chair . . .

I appreciate your invite to come to your home and am glad you have a nice place and I will come some time   this goes both ways   I have a camp in the Glacier park where the pipe is and the robe spred for you aneytime you come . . .   you wont care much for the horses   thair all quiat old mountian horses that will pack aneything from a screaming lady to a dead bear over trails that makes mountian goat nurvis   I have been mooving around so much that I have missed our home paper and never saw the artical about you   we expect to leave here in a fiew days for Great Falls   hoping you all kinds of good luck   Your friend

Rout 3 Box 223 Pasedina Califonia   C M Russell

45

KIT. CARSON that rod for the ∩
is married and quit
riding
and gin to
gaubling
he has win
a good home
here in Grate Falls
and has money in the bank he
is on the onley one of our old
Fesends that has raised from a
saddel blanket gaubler to well to do
man behind the silver box but he

all ways was lucky you know
For what hundes he held on a
blanket years ago

46

Charly Bow legs

killed at
DUPUYER
while playing
cards

Charley was killed by a beed
it was an old grudge
some years before Bow legs
shot at the breed it was
in the dark and he onley
powder bunt him of corse they
never were verry fuendly so one
day when bow legs was playing
poker he baught the drinks
the breed asked if he dident
drink to Bow legs told him
he wasent bring booze fro Inguns
and the ball opend Bow legs had
on a over coat and gouldent
get his gun quick so he cashdin

Feb 13
1918

Friend Ed

    I got a letter from you about three years ago so I thought Id hurry up and answer it. I was down on your range a year ago last October with the Eaton party and judging from what I saw Im twenty years late   the scool teachers beet me to it. those wisdom bringers surtenly wipe all the picture out of nature but I saw a fiew like the above sketch but most of them had disgarded the dress of the savige for the beautifull garments of these white brother but Ed Im glad I wint and I whish I knew those people and there past   If I savyed the south west like you Id shure paint Navys.[1]

    One camp we made I wont forget it was at a little lake in the dessert at sundown a bunch of these American Arabs droped down from the high country with about five hundred horses   most of these riders looked lik the real thing in there high forked saddles and concho belts silver ore turquis necklaces and year rings   they were all hatless some wore split pants their shirts were Navyho make but its a safe bet if we could drop back in there history they would be shy the shirt   they rode short sturrips an each packed a skin rope. They were not like the Indian I know but

48

every thing on them spelt wild people and horsemen and in a mixture of dust and red sun light it made a picture that will not let me foget Arizona

I also saw a Yabachae dance of the Navys that was wild and scary   I guess I been telling you things you already know but I like to unlode on men whos likes are the same as mine   I dont know when I will see you so I want you to write and tell me about the big camp   How is Marsh   do you ever see that Terrapin Bill Crawford   is Rogers still heeling fillyes at the follies   does he still loap up to your camp quirting himself down the hind leg with a paper   if he keeps that up hel get to be a ring tail. I wonder if Fred Stone when hes Lion hunting pulls that funny stuff of his   if he dos tell him I dont think its squar to shoot the big cat while hes Laughing

with best regards to yourself and the bunch from my best half and myself

Your friend

C M Russell

[1]Navajoes.

Mike Shanon June 17
/1923

Mike Shanon
Friend Mike

    Im a long time answering your letter but if letters were money and I was called to pay up I'd be bankrupt   Since when did you turn poet   that was good stuff   if you keep that up youl be braking into booklets and the dudes will be shy a guide but judging from the fiew poets I know dude ranglers eat oftener   I think thairl be lots of people in the park this summer and as thair are still people who like to ride I hope you and your horses have all you can handle   a machine will show folks the man made things but if people want to see Gods own country thave got to get a horse under them   In spite of gasoline the bigest part of the Rocky Mountains belongs to God and as long as it dose thairl be a home for you and your kind   to me the roar of a mountian stream mingled with the bells of a pack trane is grander musick than all the string or brass bands in the world

    Well Mike we hope to be in the park in a fiew days and if I see you we will talk   its easier than writing

    with best whishes to you and yours from me and mine.

Your friend

C M Russell

50

Edward Borein

Frend Ed

    I got your card telling of your tye up.

    Im glad your necked.

    its the onley way to hold a bunch quitter, animals are easier found in pairs than alone.

    A he bear has no home till he ties to a lady.

    The wolf is a drifter untill the she one of his kind shows him the cave under the rim rock,

    The mules in the pack trane would leave the trail and scatter, but thairs a differnt shaped track in the trail ahead.

    its the hoof marks of the lady hoss that leads her long eared lovers to camp.

    Im hoping the tie rope will never choke ore brake.

Your friend
C M Russell·

Sept 1st
1913

Friend MacKay

I suppose by this time you'r setteled down among the cliff dwelers

the seat you got in that money shack of you'rs is easier than the roost on the corall fence but I bet the looking aint as good

Our seats wasent strong for comfort but they were easier to hold than some of the boys had that left the shute   you savy those moving leather seats that so maney of the boys lost

I suppose by this time you'v bull doged every milk cow on that Ten a Fly ranch of yours   It will be hard to handle the de horned milkers but I dont think ear holts are bared

with best regards to your self and family from us all

Your friend
C M Russell

May 8
1925

Friend Harry

Im a long time thanking you for the Head dress you sent. but I never was fast
an old Dad Time aint changed my gate   the Head dress is a good one   it is certainly
a wild mans crest.

I think our red brother stole his fashion from animals and birds he knew   he
saw the sage cock dance and spred his tail fethers   that's where Mr Injun got his
dance bussel   he liked the war bonnet that the Canadian jay and the King Fisher
wore so he made himself one but the only real American dont use much stile aney
more   Unkle Sam lets him play Injun once a year and he dances under the flag that
made a farmer out of him   once nature gave him everything he wanted. now the
agent gives him bib overalls hookes his hands around plow handles and tell him its
a good thing push it along   maby it is but thair having a hell of a time prooving it.

To people who since time began never don aney thing harder
than pull a bow string ore push a skining knife nature was not
always kind to these people but she never lied to them.

The red skined men are all moste gone now Harry but if
fiew clothes and fancy ones means saviges we got lots of she ones
now and moste of them set traps for men.

Thanking you again for the head dress—good medicine to you and yours—

Your friend

Ah wah cons[1]

[1]Indian word for antelope, and Mr. Russell's Indian name.

53

C. M. RUSSELL
GREAT FALLS, MONTANA

Ed Neitsling   November 14
                                                       1923

    Friend Ed   I got the meat all right and its fine and I thank you verry much
I lost out on a hunting party   its the first fall Iv missed a hunt for many years but I
hope we will go again some time   I am better but am still using four legs   the frunt
ones are wooden

    give my regards to all Friends
    with thanks and best whishes to you

                     your friend
                     C M Russell

C M Russell

Aug 11 1912

Friend Joe   we have just received you pictures and they are shure dandys an I want to thank you for them and all so the tom tom

I was sorry that your trip wound up with such hard luck   Iv heard of men that couldent ride a coverd wagon but I suppose yours dident have a lid on. a spring seet can go higher an hit the ground harder than most bronks   I was unloded wonce my self by one an have not forgotten   I dident brak aneything but all hinges an bolts were loosened   braking your coller bone sounds reasinable enough but are you shure that Jonson dident slip in an get your scalp before you woke   you know how strong he was after suviners   aneyway I'd like to look through his getherings just to sadisfy myself. I bet hes got Dutch hair among em.

Well Joe I will close with best whishes to you and yours

Your friend

C M Russell

There was a Twister at Haver[1] that hung up a bet of fifty Dollars that hed ride a certain hoss and fan him with his hat. He might of faned him but he lost his hat an then got off to look for it.

Oct 31 1917

Friend Con

I got your letter and was glad to here from you   Im sorry you have been sick I hadent heard aney thing about it till I heard from you

in your letter you said you guessed the old timers were getting scarce up here you were right   there's a lot of them chashed in latly with in the last six months Trigg, John Mathison and Dinny Dolan all good old friends

judging by the number thats snuffed out in the last fiew years that trail is well broke and plane across the big devide   it aint had much chance to grass over

I was down at Haver last 4th of July and saw quite a nomber of our old friends Bob Stewart, K Lowrie, Bill. Mackdonna, Morman Zack Larson, Babe and Oliver Tingly, Cal Shuler, Charlie Mud, Humpy Jack Davis, Bob Malone and a fiew others Kid Price wasent thair   they say he aint verry well   from what I here he leans to much on the bar   he still eatis that old joy juice   the same old kinde that Bill Noris ust to make   three swollers and the Missouria looked lik Dog Creek   it was good

[1]Haver refers to Havre, Montana, never by any chance called other than Haver in Montana.

56

stuff to swim cattle with but when used more than a week steady its liable to bring mooving pictures the kind that nobodys stuck to see

They pulled a riding and roping contest at Haver and some of it was good old K Lowery said they was good riders all right but if theyd give him an ax and let him chop them nobs off thair saddle forks he dident think theyd stay so long

mos of our old cow puncher friends have got big famlies of groun up kids an when I look at them it makes me feel like Grand Pa

maby you dont know it Con but we got a boy at our house now he was a little two months slick ere when we put our iron on him hes a yearling past now and wer shure stuck on him his name is Jack and he reminds me of Leslie when he was a baby

well Con I colose for this time with best whishes to the three of you from us both

Your friend

C M Russell

IF NO FIND IN 10 sleeps
come Back To GREAT FaLLs

Chas. Schatzlein

BuTTe

Mont

April 7th

1912

Stuart Florida

Friend Trigg

    we are now in the land of flowers where things grow with out the help of man an when I look at its maney water wayes it is easy to understand why this was a favorit hangout for all sea holdups of the old days on these shores maney a ship changed her captions an he who lost command left his bones on the sands of Floridas shore

    well Trigg I will tell you all about it soon

    with best whishes to you all

Your friend

C M Russell

58

C. M. RUSSELL
GREAT FALLS, MONTANA

April 4 1922

Georg Calvert

Friend Georg   we were all glad to here from you   Frank Linderman and I went fishing the other day   the Ocean was pulling what the sea folks call a ground swell   it was the swellist thing Iv been to in California   Bill Hall and his quartett usto sing rocked in the cradel of the deep calm and peacefull is my sleep   I was rocked all right but I wasent calm inside ore out and I dident sleep   Bills song was all right an it sounded good floating over the mohoginy about a thousand miles from salt water if I remember right I usto get in on the base but I couldent do it now and hold my dinner   that old bunch were all right but its a sinch non of them ever fished for mackril ore road a ground swell   Frank lives next door but he and his fambly leave for home in a fiew days   we expect to leave about the first of may   I will tell you all about Calif when we get home

with best whishes to you all from the three of us

Your friend

C M Russell

59

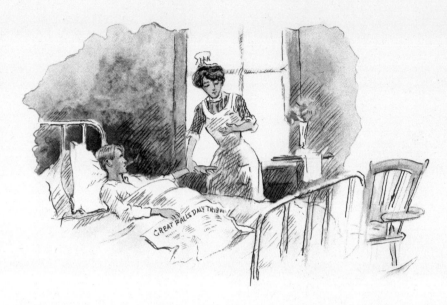

Aug 30
1908

Friend Percy

I was verry sorry to here of your sickness but by this time you have been trimed an if you are like I was you feeal a hole lote easyer in mind if your intearer dond feel just right

trouble shore com to you in bunches

it was tough enough when you tuck the antlers. but stepping off the goat onto the meet block is piling it up on you plenty an Im sending all that cheep stuff sinpothy I got on me   this is shure the age of impruvement an it looks like most men has to be made over   of corse I am glad to loose my apendex but I hope thers no more improvements to be made on my anatomy but I suppose we should bee thankfull that we dident live in the age when our Fore Fathers tailes became diseased an usless so were forsed to have them removed with a stone ax an I suppose if the patient was timid he was put to sleep with a club

there is not much news to tell up here an as we expect to be home in a fiew days I will close with best whishes hoping soon to see you

Your friend
C M Russell

Mar 4 1914

Friend Bill we received your letter and was shure glad to here from you London is quite a sisabol camp and has many things of Interist

I took in a futurist show the other day that skined any thing Iv seen one of the Futes led me around an explaned making it as clear as London it self

this Fute was bilt like a wine boltle verry lady like as wore a thin beard. I think to head off regular men that might make naughty eys at him

he sprung a string of talk that sounded like them you an Mazy ust to pull off

he led me up to something in a frame that looked like an enlarged slice of spoilt summer sausig And said this is not disintegration of Simultaneousness but Dynamic dynamism. An it did look like that. Anuther he showed as near as I could make from his talk represented the feeling of a bad stomach after a duch lunch

an it mighty near turned mine but I dident smell any limburgar

Wev been to Paris stayed onely three days Saw Saven hundred miles of pictures about the same distance in restronts sevaral Churches and Nepoilans Toom. Old Nepo has been a sleep a long time but judging from the size of the stone over him an the gards a round the French are takeing no Chances on him wakeing up. no doubt his people loved him but think hes better of where he is an its a sinch every body eles is

well Bill Il tell you all about it when I see you an that wont be long

with best regards to you an Julie from us both your friend

C M Russell

April 20, 1914

Friend Percy
here I am in
Old London
an It's Sure
antique
I was up north
of the big camp
the other day
where stands
an old monistary
allso a wall built
by the romans
built I suppose
to protect them
from Dinny Doolins
fore fathers who crosed
the chanel once an
while in there bull boats
healed with chibs of black
thorne an stone axes
to pruve to the gladitors
that life wasent no lengethy
picknic
I was told that this country was
also the home range of William the Conqueror
a gentle man whos history would make Sitting Bull
look like Brother Van

I found a pack of woods
that was realy lonsum
an I couldent help but
wonder what would
happen if the wheel
of time would slip
her cogs an slide
back to the tenth
sentury like
Mark Twains yankie

A fine chance I'd a
stood in this timber
afoot
if Bill Conk an
his bunch of
killers bad of
rode on to me
dressed in thin
steel chain union
suits
their d ben nothing
for me but take
my hat off an make
a squaring talk
or sing God save
the King

Well Percy
I will have to
Close as we are
going out in the country
with best wishes from
us both to you and yors
Your friend
C M Russell

Address Dore Gullery
35 New Bond St
London

Feb 24 1916

Friend Trigg

    we are still in camp back of the stock yards   its about thirty two years since I first saw this burg. But I remember that morning well. I was armed with a punch pole a stock car under me loded with grass eaters   I came from the big out doores and the light smoke and smell made me lonsum.

    The hole world has changed since then but I have not   Im no more at home in a big city than I was then an Im still lonsum

    If I had a winter home in Hell and a summer home in Chicago I think Id spend my summers at my winter home   There might be more people there but there couldnt be more smoke   But there is lots of good people here   maby it aint there fault

    I suppose Great Falls will be lik Cicago some day but I won't be there

    well Trigg I here the snow is all gon an I know youl miss it but youl have to bear it   You might arrange to join som poler expodation

    With best whishes to yourself Mrs Trigg Miss Josephine the chickons gold fish and bird

    This gose for both of us

Your friend
C M Russell

C. M. RUSSELL

GREAT FALLS, MONTANA

June 30
1914

Friend Joe

I heare you and
your better half are in
Harlam   my wife and I leave
here to morrow for Miles City but will be
back the 6 of July and I want you both
to come to our camp on your way
to the park   I hope you are having a good
time   if you happen to come here before
I get back go to the house   my nephew is there
and will take care of you Your friend C M Russell

65

Friend Trigg as I am lonsum to night an far from my range I thaught it might help some to write you just think I am in a camp of

Friend Trigg

    as I am lonsum to night an far from my range I thought it might help some to write you   just think I am in a camp of four millions an I guess I know about eight it makes me fell small It makes it strong d——— small the whits are shure plentyfull

    Nancy and I took in a Chinees theator the other night I guess it was good the Chinks seemed to think so, but for me it was a little better than grand opra the way those Mongoliens were painted up would make our Indian grind his teeth

with envy thair shure a scary looking bunch   baring this and a fiew other shows
I havent seen much since I been here

but I did have a good time at the Fair the most interesting to me were the
people of the Philipines especially the Iggeroties   these folks are verry primitive
forging there own weapons an weaving there own cloth but you will notice from
this sketch that the latter industry dos not take up much of thair time as there
wasent enough cloth in the hole camp to upholster a cruch   they are verry small
but well bult pople   an judging from the way they handle the spere or assiga if
they ever lern to handle the new gun Uncle Sam is liable to have trouble corraling
em   their sirtenely a snakey looking artical an they say they aint sadisfide with no
puney suvinere like a scalp but take the hole top peace from the Adams apple up

Well Trigg, hows everything in the Falls   I havent heard from there since
I left onely through Nancy an that don't tell me much of the bunch I mix with
but we expect to start home in three weeks so Il soon know.

With regards to everybody in Montana

Your friend
C M Russell
If you get time write

May 12
1920

Hello Will James

I got your letter and sketch and from it and other worke I have seen of yours in the Sunset I know you have felt a horse under you. Nobody can tell you how to draw a horse ore cow

I never got to be a bronk rider but in my youthfull days wanted to be and while that want lasted I had a fine chance to study hoss enatimy from under and over   the under was the view a taripan gits   The over while I hoverd ont the end of a Macarty rope was like the eagle sees grand but dam scary for folks without wings . . .

James, you say you havent used color much   dont be afraid of paint   I think its easier than eather pen ore pensol

I was down in Cal this winter and saw som fine back ground for cow pictures roling country green with patches of poppies and live oak   mountian ranges with white peaks that streach away to no where   I have never seen this kind of country used in cow pictures   Why dont you try it . . .

James as I said before use paint but dont get smeary   let sombody elce do that   keep on making real men horses and cows   of corse the real artistick may never know you but nature loving regular men will and thair is more of the last kind in this old world an thair the kind you want to shake hands with . . .

With best whishes to yourself and any who know me

Yours

C M Russell

June 17
1918

Friend Berners

I got your long letter and was glad to here from you an Im coming back fast for me with my short paper talk caus I know you must be lonsum in that medison camp Its a wonder them plumbers dident want to put a new pump in you. but from what you tell me that medison man looked through you with out lifting the lid an tells you that laying down is the best thing for you   its no easy game but seeing Sippys such a good guesser youd better play his hunch an if its laying down you need Lake McDonald is the best bed ground in the world and my lodge is open and the pipe lit for you and yors   you know that Lake country sings the cradle song to all who lay in her lap

Old Rip Van snoozed twenty years but if Hank Hudson would open a blind pig in our big hills with one shot of his suthing surip aney human with insomnia could beet Rips record . . .

with best whishes from my best half and me to you and yors

Your friend

C M Russell

69

Feb 4th
1902

Senitor Paris Gibson
Dear Friend

no dought you will bee suprised to here from me but if you are like myself when in St Louis you will be glad to here from aney one in Montana   As I am a verry poor writer I will make a kind of Injun letter mostly pictures

I went to see the big man the other day who was on exhibition at Luthurs hall he stood seven feet ten inches and a half   he was shure big and farley bilt but his countenance appeared to bee warped caused I supose by beeing up in the wether   his

right eye looked up bear gulch while his left survade lower alkali creek   the man that owned him said he was verry inteligant but all we got is his word for it . . .

I saw Jim Dunivan the other day   Jim looks good but the gamblers dont think so   speaking of gamblers reminds me several years ago when games were wide open   I sat at a faryo layout in Chinook   the hour was lat an the play light   a good deal of talk passed over the green bord   the subject of conversation was the Indian question   the dealor Kicking George was an old time sport who spoke of cards as an industry   he I believe was born in Missouria but came to Colorado with his folks when he was a yearling an had never left the shaddoes of the rockyes   the Kicker alloud an Injun had no more right in this country than a Cyote   I told him what he said might be right but there were folks coming to the country on the new rail road that thaught the same way about gamblers an

70

he wouldent winter maney times till hed find out the wild Indian would go but would onley brake the trail for the gambler

My prophecy came true   we still have the gambler but like the cyote civilization has made him an outlaw . . .

Speaking of Indians. I understand there is a man back in your camp Jones by name who has sent out orders to cut all the Indians hair   if Jones is stuck to have this barber work done he'd better tackle it himself as no one out here is longing for the job   the Indians say whoever starts to cut thair hair will get an Injun hair cut and you know that calls for a sertean amount of hide   they clame it makes it handier to trim legons with

Bridgman who is agent at Belnap isent worring much as he owns about as much hair as a Mexicon dog an thair fixed for hair about like a sausage   the Great Falls Daly Leader has a standing bet up of twenty to one he won't loose aney.

Well Senitor as I am all up on news I will close the deal

Hers How

With best wishes Your friend

Sep 4
1908

Friend Holland

I have received sevral letters from you an I guess its time Im answering

news are short up here an I havent seen Apgar for a day or two so I havent got much to right about

tell Littel Sunshine the blood hounds have eat the last Ladrone blood raw an are now taking there seastia an the Don after a firce struggle was swollod by an alla-gator. our hero spyed the reptile but to late an noting its sweled an after dinner look rased his trusty rifal an pirced its brane after another firce strugle it sank to the depth of the lagoon with its lothsum repast never to rase again after one long sad look our hero turned an sadly retraced his steps an marryed the widow under the spreding palms while the sweet voised pelicons sang the wedding march

72

things are verry quiet up here   since the folks left there is onley seven of us now conting the two chickons an as bakon is getting scarce I belive they will not be with us long

We have just returned from a trip to the glacier an had good wether an a fine time   the wether since has been rany an cold up to the last fiew days   it is now fine   tell Miss sun shine that the lake is still warm in spite of the cold wether

I hope Mrs Holland is getting all the tomaters I mean tommotoes she wants

people are leaving the lake every day for there homes an we will soone be getting ready our selvs

one ore two skunks have taken up quarters under the house an seem to like the place al so a number of montian rats have mooved in an by the noise they make Iv a hunch my night watches are sleeping on gard As soon as dark comes the new comers goes to work all hands   the skunks practis two steps and barn dances on the porch or in the kitchen   the rats dont seem to like our roof   all night long thair bussy making it over occasionaly stopping to gether up tooth brushes leaving rocks sticks ore old bones in exchange   they are traders who belive a fair exchange is no robery the great horned owl in the seaders at intervals askes who   no one knows so receiving no answer he keeps it up all night an at day brak flies away in disgust but returnes the next night with the same question   its to bad someone cant tell him

Well Holland as I cant think of aney more foolishness I will close with best wishes to you all

Your friend
C M Russell

November 23
1921

Guy. Weadick
T/S Ranch
Longview
Alberta

Friend Guy

I got your letter and am glad to here you are doing so well with your ranch it pleases me plenty to know that thair is so maney men and wimen that will quit a gas wagon and a good road and ore wilen to look at the world with a horse under em. and where you live Guy if theyl step in the middel of a hoss you can show folks the top of America the wildest the bigest and for a Nature Lover the best part of it

In tame countrys on a good road an autos all right but if your hunting for aney thing wilder than a Doctor take a horse

I suppose by this time your on the rode   Im sending you a book which I hope you enjoy   My wife and I leave for Denver tommorrow morning so this is a buisy camp   we will returne in about two weeks

Thanks for the Invite to viset the $\frac{T}{S}$ Ranch   we might do that some time   with best whishes to you and yours from us all

Your friend
C M Russell

74

May 1 1921

Friend Ed

    Mame wrote you a fiew days ago that we would make you a visit but the way things have turned we cant make it   we thought we could hold our hous another week but as thair is another party wants to get in we have to leave so we will have to put our viset off for another year   we leave here a week from to day   I wish you could com up to Montana this summer   if you do you know where my camp is   I have seen Bill Rogers quite often   met Dug Fairbanks Neal Hart Buck Conners and several other moovie folks   maney of them know you. I also saw Jim Minnick he wanted to be rememberd to you

    With best whishes to you and yours

from all of us

Your friend

C M Russell

Just got a paper saying Marchand is dead

old time
Center fire
man

Joe De Young

I received your letter
also model of puncher
an photo of rider you modeled
I think they were good your horse was
a little short in the back but if you will
study proportion you will come out all right
most range horses measure the same, from the
top of the head to middle of the withers
would measure the same as from there back
to the coupling teach
study your saddle horse he will tell you
more than I could tell you in a thousand years

The picture of your Father and I with the bunch in the Silver Dollar was no good   it was so blured you could hardly tell one man from annother

You will find enclosed a photo of my self and friend   I have riddin this old boy nearly 15 years so you see hes a has been

the saddle was made in 1888 by Meany of Cheyenne   it is the old time Vacala tree   the spurs I ware Iv had for 32 years   the rawhide ranes 30 and I have been in Montan nearly 34 years   so you see the picture shows a bunch of old has beens

Yores

C M Russell

Give my regards to your Father

C. M. RUSSELL

GREAT FALLS, MONTANA

Mr Ralph Kendall

Dear Mr Kendall

a guess you think its about time I said
thank you for the book you sent me
I ingoyed the book verry much
and since I red it I know why you love
pictures you are a word painter your self
betwine the pen and the brush there is little
difforence but I belive the man that makes
word pictures is the greater

Kendal you have travled lifes trails with your
eyes open you have laughed and al so
cryed for in the book of life they are
not all funny pictures

I hope you write more your country
holds maney storyes

with best whishes to you and
Yours and thanking you again

C M Russell

Pan handle Jack

killed at
Gild Edge
by a Saloon man Pan handle
gave his gun to the buze boss
then got drunk an wanted it
back the buze boss refused
an panhandle got a winchester
and come back but it was
another cose of slow

P. P. Johnson

killed in his ~~saloon~~
Saloon by night watchman
at Lewistown Jonson made
his talk that he was
going to shoot up this
watch man but when the
time come P.P was soked and
was slow delivern the led

Frank Brown
Friend Frank

April 4
1926

I received your nice long letter and was glad to here from you   this is the bigest moovie camp in the world   thair are more two gun men here now than the history of the west from north to south ever knew

I was at a studio the other day   they were making a dance hall seen   this dance Hall made aney I ever saw an Iv seen some that wasent real gentile but this one made Chicago Joes look like a Kindergarden and if I rember right Joe dident run a young ladys finishing school   if the old west had of been as tough as the mooves make it theyd be runing buffalo yet on the Great Falls flat yet   Jew Jake and Pike Sandusky were easy to get along with compared with these hair trigger moovie gun fighters I wouldent bet how good theyd be up aganst the reel thing but with blanks they look mighty nasty

Frank I see in the paper your going to take a hand in the straw hat perade   I hope you and the bunch have good luck but dont go to far with a straw hat   you might want to trade for a buffalo overcoat

Frank this country brags on its climet but the Cal booster dont tell that it also has chills   the old fashon kind that shakes and when it shakes it dont leave much but climet and no climet is much good that houses wont stand in   an Ingun lodge might be good but thairs no lodge pole pine in this country

with best whishes to your self and Great falls

Your friend
C M Russell

May 14 1914

Friend Holland

We received your letters and were shure glad to get them

We are one night out from England right now

An altho Im glad I went I did not shed maney tears leaving the home of my Ansesters

I find the Russells were pritty plenty in this land theres Great Russell St Russell Squar Hotel

Sir Russell entring the Kings Coart

Russell an all kinds of Russells in England   Iv been a littel doubtfull about my folks. I always had an Idar that the Russell tree was a scrub. but the other day I was told that Sir Sombody Russell was led to the block an had the upper end of his back bone removed by the Kings ax man who was a bussyer man them days than Fred Piper ever was on saterday night. this loping off of Sir Russells Head makes it sinch he was a Nobel man. as in those dayes scrubs mostley cashed in in bed. A verry unrefined way of quitten So Holland if I happen to pass you on the street an you feel a chill like an ice wagon had gon by dont blame me   its the blood of the Nobility Iv got in me   It might pay you to come over an round up this Histori- cal range but as you claime I belive Scotch blood youd have to work the country further north where I dont doubt youd find Hollands onery enough to mix with the King an as near as I can make from history If a man

Sir Russells Departure

was a fighter an could count enough notches he was Be Knighted by the King or Be Headed. eather way his pedigree was safe an all those to whome he left his name which was generly all he had to leave were of noble blood ...

from your friend

C M Russell

81

Friend Kid I received your letter
an was glad to here from you
I have often wandered where you
were since I saw you in the land
of these pople

I was afraid

the Puralyes
had taken you in, but I am glad
you beet them to the line
and are safe   this side

the old Rio Grand. wet clathes in the
United Stats are often more comfurtibal than
dry ones in Mexico

I saw Jim two years ago in the big camp   he was punching cows at the Hipidrome an altho he was fighting Sioux every day he wasent scared up much

the last I saw of him he was thinking of crossing the creek that layes betwin New York and Londen but as I have never heard from him I dont know whether hes still in this country ore not

now kid I hope you hit this country an if you drift on to my range dont pass my camp   the latch string is out side for you and yours

With best whishes from us both to your self and wife

Your friend
C M Russell

C. M. RUSSELL,
GREAT FALLS, MONTANA.

Chas. Schatzlein
Butte
Mont

We meet again Douglas Fairbanks, alias D'Artagnan tho only on paper.

My hats of to you I have seen you under many names and you have worn them all well—an actor of action always—And now since you have back tracked the grass grown trails of history and romance I know that D'Artagnan's name will fit you as well as his clothes.

But Doug don't forget our old west. The old time cow man right now is as much history as Richard, The Lion Harted or any of those gents that packed a long blade and had their cloths made by a blacksmith.

You and others have done the west and showed it well, but theres lots of it left, from Mexico north to the Great Slave lakes The west was a big home for the adventurer—good or bad—he had to be a regular man and in skin and leather men were almost as fancy and picturesque as the steel clad fighters of the old world The west had some fighters, long haired Wild Bill Hickok with a cap and ball Colts could have made a correll full of King Arthurs men climb a tree.

Your friend

C. M. Russell

C. M. RUSSELL

GREAT FALLS, MONTANA

Apral 30
1922

Friend Georg

Im a long time answering your letter but you know I never was rapid with ink
I hear its been cold up home   well it aint had nothing on the oringe belt   Its don
everything but snow down here   Iv been cold so long now Im numb   Its kind a
like the first stages of freesing to death   its painless   Georg if you ever figer on
wintering down here take my advise bring a stove and some sand coole ore belt creek
with you   ladyes ore still waring furs but nothing elce much but paint   from now
on nobody can tell me that he humans or more hardy than shes   if a baby doll tuck
a notion she wanted an Esquemaw she'd slip on som gaus and lace and with a powder
puff and lip stick she'd start for the Pole and freeze aney dog runner in his cariboo
capote to death that ever traveled the Great Slave providen she don't run short of
power ore rouge.

The wethers fine right now. Little Jack is shure haven a good time   he gets
lots of out doors   the countrys open here and all we do is range heard him

We start home May 14 and when I get home Il tell you all about Cal   With
best whishes to you all including your Grand son from the three of us

Your friend
C M Russell

R 3 Box 223 Pasidana Cal

The trail is long it is good if Seldon Writes makes maney moccasins an when the grass comes let him travel to the big hills where the sun sleeps

Three times have the dogs howled at my lodge door while I ate smoked an slept by the fire of Seldom Writes but never has the grass been bent my way by his moccasins has Seldom Writes grown fast to his shell like the littel water people that live about him

(A letter written to Will Crawford, an artist friend of his living in New York. The man on the horse is Charlie Russell and the man painting the robe is Will Crawford. One represents the Western Indian; the other the Eastern.)

The trail is long   it is good if Seldom Writes makes maney moccasins an when the grass comes let him travel to the big hills where the sun sleeps

Three times have the dogs howled at my lodge door while I ate smoked an slept by the fire of Seldom Writes but never has the grass been bent my way by his moccasins   Has Seldom Writes grown fast to his shell like the littel water people that live about him.

C M R   1909

July 9th 1910

Hellow Dutch

how are you   we expect to go to the lake about the 15th an we want you and your wife to com up

be shure and bring your paint box   I expect Goodwin soon an if you come we will shure do some painting   are you doing aney modling these days

I here Cut Banks married   how dos he work in double harness

I hope you dident loose on the fight   theres shure a sore bunch over here . . .

I had a good time East and made a littel money   will tell you all about it when we meet   with best whishes to you both from us both

your friend

C M Russell

THE BILTMORE SALON
DEDICATED TO WESTERN ART

March 27
1924

Dear Miss Josephine

Thank you for the birth day card

Old Dad Time trades little that men want   he has traded me wrinkles for teeth stiff legs for limber ones   but cards, like yours, tell me he has left me my friends and for that great kindness I forgive him,

Good friends make the roughest trail easy

Mame and I are much better   a fiew days more and I think Il shed the stick Jack seems to like school.

The above sketch is before Cal. was taken by the Iowans

with best wishes to you and your Mother and Miss Furnald

Your friend

C M Russell

Dec 12 1924

Bill Gollings

Friend Bill

Some time ago I received your letter and photos of your self with the long bow Joe tells me you skined your red brothers at thair own game. Bill you aint Injun thats a sinch   maby thair was some Gollingses with Robin Hoods band   Bob and his friends were fast with the long bow

If youd lived where you do now in 1846 Francis Parkman in his book would have told of a white man living with Ogillallahs that packed a long bow and a robe painted by him would bring twenty Poneys   a shield cover was worth five wimen painted by Robe pictures   that was what the Ogillallahs called him   he was rich received no bills and paid no taxes

Aint it hell Bill what we missed by coming late   I supose by this time your meats all jurked and hides all taned   Im back on my feet again and in pritty good shape   Joe is here with me   hes doing lots of painting

with best whishes   Your friend

C M Russell

C. M. RUSSELL

GREAT FALLS, MONTANA

November 9, 1924

Ed. Neitzling

Friend Ed again I thank
you for that fine hind quarter of deer
it is shure fine thair is no meat as good
as the wild for me

I am sorry you dident have a good time on
your hunt

this fall makes two years Iv missed

I am as you know a harmless hunter but
I shure like to git out with a good bunch
the old rumitism I dont know whethr that
the way to spell it or not but it is still with
me but by next fall I hope to git out
with the same good bunch we shure had
a good time

with best regards to you and
all friends

thanking you
your friend
C M Russell

90

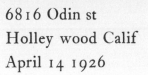

6816 Odin st
Holley wood Calif
April 14 1926

Ted Abbott
Friend Ted

. . .

Im now camped among the move cow boys This kind dont ride Sircle or night gard   their remutha travels in a truck and their wagon is a cafeteria   he dont have to know cows or brands but the move cow boy must have plenty of guts an no head

It takes sevral kinds to make a hero on the screen   the beautiful cow boy that makes love till the reformers want to burn the picture houses aint the same man that spures his horse of a thirty foot rim rock into the water and swims three miles to save his sweet hart from a band of out laws aint the same   they usto say that camres wouldent lye but Holleywood has quired that talk

this feller that goes off the rim-rock is what they call a double
Som actores donte use them. . . .

Most of the moovie men Iv met are good fellers   Maby they aint got much under thair hats but an Old Injun told me once that real good brave men lived in thair harts not thair heds and I belive my red brother was right

Well Ted . . . if my good whishes ar aney good to you Im sending them all that goes for every thing Famely cows horses aney thing waring the three duce iron

Your old friend

C M Russell

91

Magpie. Wheres that man going
Crow. Dam fi know ask the horse

Sept 24
1914

Friend Bill Krieghoff

    I dont have to tell you that the above sketch is not a chees eater carring despatches for Bill Hohenzollern the second

    This rider's name is also Bill an clames german breeding   he eats every thing a dutchman will which mighty nere proves it an by the gate he went I think hes Bill the first   Duck Leg if you could onley git across to them fighting folks of yours with that horse and lead a charge there woldent trees enough in France to hold the Frog eaters

    well Bill were still here at the Lake but are leaving day after tommorrow for home   we have had fine wether till the last two weeks   Its been raining mighty steady an now the country sogy as a wet blanket an its cold an Bill you know what that meens to the wood getters   Auston an I both miss you verry much   Mame an I went over to Kalispell on our way to Flat head Lake where we visited Linderman and his folks who were camped there   on our way back we bumped in to your old pard little Artie Larivy   every body inquired after Willie

Bob Benn and his wife spent a couple of days with us at the lake   Mrs Benn spoke of the Arte talk you sawed of to her   she said it was verry interesting but she dident savy only about half of it   I guess you sprung some of that Mazzy on her Bill

I heard it so often I can almost handel it my self but don't know what it meanes yet.

Joe Scheuerle and his wife were here with us a fiew days and we had a good time

We all so saw Mr and Mrs Crudson at the foot of the lake wating for the boat they were on there way through the park

well Bill I will close with best whishes to you and Jule also all friends from us all

Your friend

C M Russell.

Ronan
Flathead
Resirvation
1908

Friend Fred com on an bring
the bunch the lids off up here
there playing on the first floor
black jack an Monty wide open
be carful an dont tip it off to non
of them Morilests
                with regardst to the bunch
                    your freind
                        C M Russell

94

Feb 16 1919

Friend Bollinger

I received your good long letter and was glad to here from you and that you had a good hunt and brought in meat   but your rong when you think the absence of Mrs B[1] had aney thing to do with my not showing up on that hunt. but I had a hunch you and Lewis would hold that agin me   it would be a safer bet to play me the other way   four Jacks and a Queen is a good hand in stud poker but the same number of hes and a she like Mrs B aint a lucky combination and a deer hunt might turn to man slaughter   Some morning that camp might look like one of Bill Harts moovies   The onley difference some of the performers wouldent act no more   the above sketch would go good in the moovies but it would look like hell in the Great Falls ore Davenport papers   Romance is a beautiful lady that lives in the book case who can pull aney thing from a cold deck to murder and get away with it but shes got a homely sister Reality by name that hangs around all the time

this old girl aint so lucky   let som man make a killing over her and the Judge tells him where hes going and nobody knowes his address after that

Mrs B dident take the picture   som body in New York bought it   the price was three hundred   my oils run from six hundred to two thousand

With best whishes from all the Russells to you all

Your friend

C M Russell

[1] "Mrs. B" refers to a lady in no way related to either the writer or the recipient of the letter. —*Editor*.

Novembr 27
1924

Walter Coburn
Friend Walt

I just received your letter   got the magisines som time ago   liked both the storyes   your cow punchers seemed real to me   they were like those I knew in old days. thair are maney western writers these days but fiew of them knew the range   I red a story the other day   in it the punchers wore bandanas round thair necks   the bandana came and belonged to the sod buster and generly toped bib overalles   I never knew a cow hand to ware aney thing but silk if it wasent the warer thought it was   in late years Iv seen riders that looked like this sketch   this kind are generly found around a soft drink parlor   I don't know whether its CoCo Cola ore mapel nut sunday that works his legs the wrong way but I do know no cow puncher I ever knew if he was going to ride a snake would take aney thing soft as a brave maker   this cococola soke can tell whats the matter with a ford by the nois it makes but he wouldent know that a wet cold horse with a hump in his back is dangerious   Shaps spurs and boots and big hat dont make riders   neather dos bib overalls and caps make pictures ore storyes

This kind I knew they are almost extinct now   a foot he was mighty near harmless but with a horse under him he wase never lame   he is not used much these days but in days before the wires the west needed him

Your modling looked good   stay with it   its a lot easier than drawing

Tell Jim Fisher I have heard Ted Blue talk about him   I am glad he writes well   all old timers who can write should tell what they know of the old west

I will watch for your storys in Adventure   that magazine is my favorite

with best regards
Your friend
C M Russell

Friend Perc

    you are right iv reached another station The road has been long but my friends have made it a pleasant one   And it is goot to know when Im past the half way ranch that my friends still greet me at the stations beond

    Best whishes to you and yours

                                        Your friend
                                            C M Russell

                                        Pasadina Cal
                                        March 27 1920

97

March 20 1918

Dear Brother Van

I received an invation to your birthday party from Reverend Bunch an am more than sorry that I cant be their but Im on the jury

I think it was about this time of year thirty sevon years ago that we first met at Babcocks ranch in Pigeye bason on the upper Judith   I was living at that time with a hunter and trapper Jake Hoover who you will remember   He and I had come down from the south fork with three pack horses loaded with deer and elk meet which he sold to the ranchers and we had stopped for the night with old Bab, a man as rough as the mountians he loved but who was all hart from his belt up and friends ore strangers were welcom to shove there feet under his table   this all welcom way of his made the camp a hangout for many homeless mountian and prairie men and his log walls and dirt roof semed like a palice to those who lived mostly under the sky

the eavning you came there was a mixture of bull whackers hunters and prospecters who welcomed you with hand shaks and rough but friendyl greetings

I was the only stranger to you so after Bab interduced Kid Russell he took me to one side and whispered

boy says he I don't savy maney samsingers but Brother Van deels square

and when we all sat down to our elk meet beens coffee and dryed apples under the rays of a bacon grease light. these men who knew little of law and one among them I knew wore notches on his gun   men who had not prayed since they nelt at their mothers knee bowed there heads while you, Brother Van, gave thanks and when you finished some one said Amen   I am not sure but I think it was a man who I heard later was ore had been a rode agent . . .

With best wishes from my best half and me   Your Friend

C M Russell

This is the departure of my Great Great Geat Grand dad
some of the Kings men cane to see him off but were a littel late
Grand dad went for his batth some of his friends told him the
Climate in America would lengthen his life an no doubt it did

April 12 1914

Friend Trigg

here we are in the land of your birth al so the home of my forfathers but I think mine left early and judging from history I dont blame them   America with its red men was some scary but peacful compared with this, scalped men have been known to live but nobody can thrive with out a head

up to a hundred years ago, a man was safer in a skin lodge in the wilds of America than the stone castles of this mans land but this is a quiet country now peacful and law loving   maby this gent cleaned out the bad wanes   I saw his tools at the old tower an from looks Id say Hed been som busy

Im pritty lame on history but its a sinch bet this gent was the cause of maney a early hom seeker in the new world as an emigration booster he had Jim and Lewie Hill beat to a fair you well

Well Trigg I have seen many strange things all verry interesting but I am shure home sick and hungry for home grub   I dont belive theres a biscut or hotcake in the British Iles this is shure a cold bread country its supper time right now an Id lik to be with my feet under your table   tell Miss Josephine Id eaven eate some of her salid an I never did yearn for salid . . .

Best regards to You and Yors
Your friend
C M Russell

99

My Brother we are both from the
big hills
But our fires have been far apart
We met in a strange land
Lonesumness makes strong friends
of shy strangers
In this big camp where the
lodges hide the sun and its
people rube sholders but do not
speek
your pipe was mine
It is good our harts are the
same
To Ed. Borein
From his friend
C M Russell

1916

C. M. RUSSELL
GREAT FALLS, MONTANA

July 25 1911

Friend Eaton

It has been a long time since I threw the dimond   I think it was the last trip. My Pardner a farm raised man couldent think of coffe without milk so we blew for som caned cow juce. It was the old kind you know the eagle brand I belive an I think it came from that bird   its a sinch it never flowed from any animal with hornes to make a long story short it got loos on us. an I dont have to tell you what happened when it started wandering through our pack   we had milk in every thing but our coffe

Eaton we would like mighty well to join you but Iv got so much work I cant brake away

Thanking you for the invition
with best whishes from us both

your friend
C M Russell

Dec 4 1922

Charles Furlong

My hats to you
Who has traveled on your humped backed mount
a country where mans trails began
You have ridden old trails and blazed new ones
and with word and picture have told the new world
I enjoyed your book Let Her Buck very much

With best wishes
Your friend
C M Russell

Friend Schatzlein

since seeing you in those breed garmants its hard to belive youre dutch   it shure dont take much trimings to put you back to the savage

I have been taken for a white headed breed sevral times myself but youv got me skined

I dont think theres a drop of Injun blood in you but I wouldent bet on it for the early comers to America were all traders   the first whites in Verginia swaped tobbaco for wives an folks now that clame kin to Pocahontas are mighty chesty over it

taking history for it the dutch were som traders an it might be that your Great Great Great Grand Dad swaped for a red Wife   from your looks Id advise not looking to far back in your famely tree.

when are you all coming over with regards

your friend

CMR

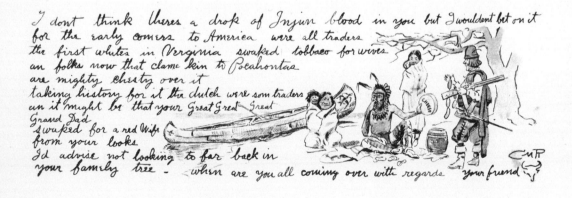

Friend Con   Oct 28 1910

    I received your letter an was glad to here from you but am sorry you dont like that appel country   its pritty hard for an old cow puncher lik you to fall to frute rasing   picking appels aint verry exciting   I like appels an so do you but if they will give me the country back the way it was Il agree to eat dryed frute the rest of my life but theres onely a fiew of us that feel that way.

    I have been inquiring about a hay ranch but as aney kind of hay sells for $25 a ton they dont seem stuck to sell out but Il keep my eye open   I shure wish you could get a ranch nere here

    You spoke of Jonny Lee in your letter   I was one of his pallbearer   he went quick   a cow puncher from Browning that was at the funeral told me he was sick onely a fiew minuts   he had just com home from a dance an his hart quit   I hated to see poor Jonny go but if my friends have to go I want them to go fast

    Goodwin an I got home all safe   we had the horses shod at Gelida   they stood like plow horses an since I got hack they have neather one scared at aotoes ore street cares   they act like they were raised on gasilene

    I was down town the other day an met Cap Tool Tom Daley   we were standing in front of the Mint an I asked them if they knew the horse in front of the Silver Doller   he was standing with his head down asleep with skunk wagons all around him snorting tooting and blowing   when I told them it was Dave they pritty near called me a lyar an I had to show them the "three E" to proove it

    with best whishes from us both to yourself Mrs Price and Leslie

Your friend
C M Russell

W. M. Armstrong

Los Angeles Calif

Friend Armstrong

I call you this as I count all those who love the old west friends

The brown hurds and wild men that Parkman knew and told of so well have gon   The long horned spotted cows that walked the same trails their humped backed cousins made have joined them in history and with them went the wether worn cow men   They live now onley in bookes. The cow puncher of Forty years ago is as much history as Parkmans Trapper. The west is still a great country but the picture and story part of it has been plowed under by the farmer   Prohabition maby made the west better But its sinch bet Such Gents as Trappers Traders Prospectors Bull-whackers Mule Skinners Stage drivers and Cowpunchers dident feed up on cocola or mapel nut sundais

To make sketches in Francis Parkman's books has been a pleasure to me

When I read his work I seem to live in his time and travel the trails with him

Whishing you and yours health and happyness

Your friend

C M Russell

Pat Rily was killed while sleeping
of a dunk at grass range

Pat took a buze joint and
after snoking the place up and
an running every body out till
it looked like it was for rent
fell a sleep the buze boss
gets a gun aneores back an
catcher Pat slumbrin pat
never woke up but quit
snoring

Charly Cugar quit pinsalching
and went into the cow business
for him self his start was

a couple of cows and
a worke bull each
cow had from 6 to 8
calves a year people
didnt say much
till the bull got to having
calves and then they made it
so disagreable that lcharly quit
the business and is now making
horse hair bridles they say he
hasent changed much but wares
his hair verry short an diss
dresses aufully loud

Feb 24
1909

Friend Sweet

No dought you will be supprised to here from an old night hawk like me but the older I get the more I think of the old days an the times we had before the bench land granger grabed the grass   there was no law aginst smoking sigeretts then an no need of a whipping post for wife beeters   the fiew men that had wives were so scared of loosing them they generley handeled them mighty tender. the scacity of the females give them considerbal edg those days   I never licked no women but Im shure glad I beet these morilests to the country   its hard to guess what they would have don to me. Chances are Id be making hair bridles now for smoking sigeretts or staying up after twelve oclock. but they got here to late to hed of my fun an as I am real good now I aint worring much

but what I started to say is this.

the last time I saw you I think you said you had a photo that was taken at White Sulpher of your self Jim Macoy and I   if so I wish you would send it up to me and I will have a copy made of it and return the origanal or you might have your town photographer make some copyes and send me the bill

with best regards to your self and Wife

Your friend

C M Russell

remember me to all friends

HÊRS A LIVE ONE

May 3d 1907

Friend Percy

I am still on dear old brodway among the cliff dwelers every body lives high here but they aint got me skined much I'm camped above timber line myself

I was down at Madison Square gardon the other day an met Cody he's lost most of his hair in the London fog but his back locks are still long the show was good real cow boys an Indians

I learn here that punchers wore red shirts an indians go to ware strung with slay bells but baring these detals the show was all right

this reminds me of central ave but laying all jokes aside Il take our streets bumps an all N Y with cabs under ground an sky sayling car lines is all right for them that like her, but I know a town with two mil of track an a fiew hacks thats swift anough for me give me the camp where I savy the people

well Percy it wont be long till Il be with you an Il tell you all about it

with best regards to your self and friends

Your friend

C M Russell

C. M. RUSSELL

GREAT FALLS, MONTANA

W. M. Armstrong

Augast 14
1922

Friend Armstrong

I guess you think its about time I cam across
with som thanks for the cow puncher book
I'm better than a green hand with talk   but with a pen I'm plenty
lame so I'm limping in with my thanks
Since most of the cow folks moovd to HollyWood and worke for the movies
all the cow punchers I see these dayes are on the screen
Most of the cow now are hornless ware a bell and are punched with a stool
times have changed   the old time cow puncher in the sketch above who sits in
the shade of his hoss   would run off a band of hosses hold up a coach
work a brand over   maby he wore notches on his gun
but he wouldent steal milk
from a calf

The few old raw hids left are found in a blind pig or hide in
the mountians making Moon   they have lived past thair time
they were good cow men they might have braged on thair roping and
riding but the moon shine they make cant be braged on

The cow folks I see on the screen are mighty mussy gun men
and if thair had been as many people killed in real life
as thair is on the screen with blank shells

110

I guess you think its about time I came across with som thanks for the cow puncher book   Im better than a green hand with talk but with a pen Im plenty lame so Im limping in with my thanks

Since most of the cow folks moved to Holly Wood and worke for the movies all the cow punchers I see these dayes are on the screen   Most of the cow now are hornless ware a bell and are punched with a stool

Times have changed   the old time cow puncher in the sketch above who sits in the shade of his hoss would run off a band of hosses hold up a coach work a brand over   maby he wore notches on his gun but he wouldent steal milk from a calf

The fiew old raw hids left are found in a blind pig or hide in the mountians making moon   they have lived past thair time   they were good cow men   they might have braged on thair roping and riding but the moon shine they make cant be braged on

The cow folks I see on the screen are mighty mussy gunmen and if thair had been as many people killed in real life as thair is on the screen with blank shells Its a sinch my red brothers would still be eating humped backed cows   it would have been a snap for the Injun to clean up the fiew these gun fighters left

The barbed wire and plow made the cow puncher History and the onley place hes found now is on paper   so I thank you for the book

I just returned from a fishing trip with two friends of yours Church Mehard and Walter Grange   I wish youd been with us   we went on horseback with pack animals and found good fishing   a two year old Lady brown bear called on us

Grange as you know is a ball player   he practiced in and out curves with bolders on miss bear till the lady took timber   if the animal had of been a silver tip or grizzly the sport would have gon the other way—a tree climbing contest I think

with best whishes to you and yours

from the Russells

Your friend
C M Russell

Oct 23 1907

Ho Ho Hay-ee
Friend Goodwin

I received your letter some time ago   the lion was heap good   My sketch shows a Kootnei canoe from a model H. Stanford sent me   it is made of spruce bark, rough sid in   the modle was verry rough an I could not get much from it   it has no thorts like other conoes but I think the fellow that made the modle forgot them it dont look like aney bark boat would hang together with no brace to keep her from spreding   I wish you were here now   the wether is beautifull   this sounds lik a josh but its on the square   the sun hasent hid since you left   I fineshed my roping picture an have done three black and whites two for Bronson and one for Outing.

I went to the stock yards the other day to see a beef heard from the upper sun river   there was a thousand head   pritty good heard for these days   the punchers baring a fiew bib overall boys were apritty good bunch   I knew most of the old timers so I had a good time talking over days of the open range an Im telling you there was some tolibel snakey ones rode during our talk but as the old ones knew I don most of my riding bad ones this way . . .

your friend
C M Russell

May 29/1924

Tom Kerwin   Rout 3 Box 223
Friend Tom   Pasadena Cal

    Im droping a line to let you know that I'm on my legs again but I dont travel like a colt yet. Gorge Speck wanted to bet hed hold the handels ore buy flowers for me, you tell Speck thair aint a chance, Il be the one that will let him down easy with my hat off.

    I called on [an old friend] . . . hes looking fine, is married, and has a fine home, a car, and a man to drive it. . . .

    hes on top now and Im glad of it. Hes hit som rough trails since he left Cut Bank where he started in that booze joint called The Mavorick; he played both ways from the middel when the hich rack in frount held lots of horses, he had a big bar trade, when cow punchers left, he used the back door. Fore one doller hed give his red brothers a quart of something that would mak him sing like he did in buffalo days but as thair was always enough sober ones to cash all the guns and knives it was noisy but not dangorus; It was bad booz but it dident kill aney body. I tryed it and I think maby you did Tom

    It was rough stuff made for outside men and Inguns and was agin the law to feed it to red men but now since were all inguns that old trade whisky was lemonade compared to what the whites are getting now. . . .

    give my regards to Sid and Cal and all friends   best whishes to you and your wife

Your friend

C M Russell

April 14 1914

Friend Henry

what do you think of it
this is the kind of rider that lives in
this country I see these every day an
I know its on the square cans I havent
drank a drop since I been here
how would you liker to start on sircul
with a bunch of these
I wander what would have happend if old
Pat- Jack Anderson or Jim Mcoy would have
jumped one of these on the range
these riders use as many reins on one
horse as a stage driver dos handeling
four. they tell me these men with there
muly saddels can stay in the middle
of a snakey one. but you know Hank

114

Friend Henry

What do you think of it   this is the kind of rider that lives in this country I see these every day an I know its on the square caus I havent drank a drop since I been here   How would you like to start on sircul with a bunch of these

I wonder what would have happened if old Peet-Jack Anderson or Jim Mcoy would have jumped one of these on the range   these riders use as many reins on one horse as a stage driver dos handeling fore. they tell me these men with there muly saddels can stay in the middle of a snakey one. but you know Hank Im from that state laying south of Iowa

Well Henry this is shure a old country   I was in the towar of London the other day   It is an old castle built five hundred years before Columbus found America   last Sunday I went out in the country   it looks like one big garden   everything is green   I saw small bands of sheep an one place a rider was driving four cows an as he was a boy and driving cows its a sinch he was a cow boy but all joshing aside they shure got good looking horses in this mans land   I havent seen a poor one since I landed

Well High Wood old boy Il close for this time   If you get time betwene feeding the furnace an hearding them hens of yours drop a line   I suppose your still gambling with Hinote for car fare   be carful the reformers dont grab you

with regards to you and yours

Your old friend
C M Russell

address
Dore Gallery
35 New Bond st
London
England

115

I suppose this would be an easy throw for aney of them skin string Buckaroos.

Friend Con

a fiew days ago I got your letter and one a long time ago which makes me owe you two   I rote you one since you went down to Cal but you never said you got it

Im glad you like that country and from what you say its a good one. long ago I ust to hear them senter fire long reatia Buckaroos tell about Califonia rodaros but at this late day I dident think thair was a cow in Cal that wasent waring a bell. Poor old Montana is the worst I ever seen an Iv been here forty snows   the Reformers made her dry and the Allmighty throwed in with them and turned the water of an now thair aint enough grass in the hole State to winter a prarie dog, but if the nesters could sell thair tumble weed at a dollar a tun thair all millionairs   its shure a bumper crop

I saw Jonny Rich not long ago   hes running a moovie show in Lewistown and dooing well   he says last winter when the flew hit his town the Doctor advised him to take three mouths full of booze a day to head off the sickniss   to make shure how much hes taking Jonny measurs a mouth full which he says is an eaven pint   he followes the Doctors orders to a hair and the Flew never tuched him said he felt fine all the time but after about a month of this treatment he got to seeing things that aint in the natural history. one day he saw a Poler Bear sitting on a hot stove waring a coonskin coat and felt boots eating hot tommales

I went to the stampeed at Calgary this fall and it was shure good   saw a fiew old timers some old friends of yors

Charlie Furman said a long time ago he had a horse that he was a fraid of one day hes riding this animal kinder carful with feet way out and choking the horn when suddenly with out cause this hoss starts playing peek a boo   about the second jump, Charley is unloaded among a crop of bolders an he tells me hes numb all over and feels like every bone hes got is broke in three places but when he starts coming back to life his hart gets big and all of a sudden he remembers he ain't give Con Price no wedding present so next day he saddles a gentle horse and leads peek a boo over and presents him to you

Furaman says he don't see you for quit a while but when he dos meet you you say some things that I cant put in this letter and you said if ever you married again that he needent send no presents

I am sending you a couple of pictures of Jack   Mame sent you som last winter in a Christmas pacage for Leslie but I guess you dident get them   hes shure a fine boy and loves horses   hes got a rocking horse and two stick horses an he rids the tail off the hole string   I still have a cople of old cyuses and some times I take him in the saddle with me and it shure tickles him   we may come to Cal this winter   if we do wel try and look you up. I'v got a long range cousin in that country named Philips that is runing cows down thair somewhere

Well Con I'l close for this time   with best wishes from the three of us to the three Prices

Your friend
C M Russell

C. M. RUSSELL
GREAT FALLS, MONTANA

May 18 1923

Georg Speck
Friend Gorg

    this sketch will show you Im still in Cal   I was at the beach the other day and if truth gose naked like they say it dos folks dont lye much at the sea shore   a man that tyes to a lady down hear after seeing her in bathing aint gambling much   its a good place to pick em but its sometimes Hell to hold em   this is a good country for lawyers and preachers ones tying the others untying an thair both busy

    I met Cut Bank the other day   he looked like hes in the money   hes got a real estate offis   maby hes mixing boot leg with real estate   I hear its a good blend I havent met maney of my friends down here this trip but I havent called on the Jails yet   Saw Sportecus   hes still packing a hide full   he shuck hands with about four of me and said he was glad to see us   I dont understand how he keeps away the snakes maby they dont com with this new moon   aneybody else but Sporticus would of had Crockdiles riding hyenas by this time . . . with best regards to you . . .

Your friend

C M Russell

118

Feb 25 1921

Friend Carey

Last year when I eat at the HC wagon you whisperd to me that thair was som buried treasures on your ranch that wasent no cash of the Old Spanish Bandits   But a plant of your own in days when corn and rye juice could be got for one dollor a quart   you were foxy and buried what you couldent swallow but not having the nose of the fox you couldent locate the cash   In these days of drouth there were times when it got on your nurvs. You told me you were going to organize a small band of trusted booze hounds and go prospecting   I hope you raised the cash   we got your note and was glad to here from you

with best whishes to you and yours from me and mine

Your friend

C M Russell

Hers hoping healths The hoss under you
Ahead a Long easy ride
Good water and grass
To The Top of The pass
Were The Trails cross
The Big Devide

To you and Yours
From me and mine

Your Friend
C M Russell
1924

(Card to W. M. Armstrong, Los Angeles, California.)

Hers hoping healths the hoss under you
Ahead a long easy ride
Good water and grass
To the top of the pass
Were the trails cross
        The Big Devide
                To you and yours
                From me and mine
                    Your Friend
                        C M Russell

                            1924

*Here's how to me and my friends
the same to You and Yours*

I savoy these folks

C. M. R. 1907

*Merit Flanigan married
and got a good job as
stock wispler at Glasco*

Jan 23 1924
Great Falls Mont

Jim Thornhill
Friend Jim

I got your letter and was glad to here from you   I have been layed up with siatic rumitisum for six months   I been near enough Hell to smell smoke . . .

Jim since you left thairs a lot of old cow punchers friends of yours and mine have cashed in . . . Con Price is among the senter fire men at Gilroy Califonia riding for the Gilroy Cattel Co . . . I saw Tom Daly at Selby in July   he has som oil land and cant talk nothing but oil   Old Horis Brouster is forist ranger in Glacier Park he still loves to talk about cows   he told me hed like to get out and run a wagon I told him if he did it would be a milk wagon   nearly all the cows in Montana these days are waring a bell and most of the old cow punchers that aint in Jail are making moon or boot leging

Dave Clar cam to town the other day   he got married a fiew days ago   when that lady was draging her loop it lookes to me like she dont care what steped in it Since Dave notched his gun a fiew years ago at Cut Bank he dont hang around that country much   the breed he got had friends   Dave was superstitious and Cut Bank dont look like a health resort to Davy . . .

The little picture at the head of this letter is to help you remember what snow looked like   I tryed to make it look like the country and the punchers you usto know before the grangers turned Montana grass side down   shes a has been now but wel remember her for what she was

Your friend
C M Russell

June 5
1918

Friend Tex

I got your card asking how my old hoss is   hes standing in my coral right now
but neather him nor his owner are aneything like booze   old Dad time aint hung
no improventmunts on us   Judging from your card your still in the big camp prooving to them cliff dwelers that a rope will hold things with out clothes pins   If you
ever cut Ed Borines range climb to that owls nest of his and kinder jog his memory
that he owes me som writeing   tell him I got the tapadaroes and macarthey and
thank him for me

Several months ago I got a card from you saying you was a Dad of a son. youv
got nothing on us but ours wasent waring our Iron but his brands vented so hes ours
all right and we shure love him   hes a yearling past now and it keeps us both riding
heard on him

with best whishes to your best half yourself and son from the Russell family
Your friend
C M Russell

Nolen Armstrong was
bush whacked at Culbertson
while smoking up the town
by the dupity sheriff
I am glad to say the dupity
since got the same medisn

FRANK HarTsel

Frank was bush whacked
at his ranch on warm
spring creek while pealing
potatoes for supper no one
knows ∧ who did it
he lived longenough to tell
the breed that was with him
to put out the light

Its pretty Scary at
Hollywood
Its wonderful what a man can do
with one gun if hes got blank catriages

Pasadina Califonia
March 30
1920

Friend Joe

I got your letter and paintings   they were wonderfull from an artistick stand-
point not quite bold enough in stroke. Youd have don better with a hay knife   It
would give more teck neque   maby that aint spelt right but you savvy   Thars lots
of moovie cow folks here both male and female   more he ones than thair is cows
the only cows Iv seen is the kind you moove up on with a stool an bucket

Saw Tom Mix and Bill Hart work   both treated me fine   Tom sent his
regards to you and yors   onley saw Neal Hart a fiew minuts   he also sends regards
have seen Bill Rogers work several times   Am going into the mountians with him
Sonday to see them make some real out door pictures   If you ever want to paint
frute roses ore automobiles come to this country   I forgot Bungaloos   they grow
here too   this last groath origanaly came from India where they had to be snake
and tiger proof but judging from the one we got Califonia is like Irland   well Joe
Il tell you all about it when I git home which wont be long

with best whishes to you three from we of the same nomber.

Your friend
C M Russell

THE FIGHTING CHEYENNES

The Red man was the true American
They have almost gon. but will never
be forgotten
The history of how they fought for
their county is written in blood
a stain that time cannot grinde
out
their God was the sun their Church
all out doors their only book
was nature and they knew all
its pages
          C M Russell

Jan 2
1921
Wishing You and Yours
A Happy New Year

Friend Con

I got your letter last summer and so you will know Im still living I am droping you a line   I hope you are still at Gilroy

we leave tommorrow night for New York   expect to be thair about a month   if we gethar aney coin we will go down to Calafonia. . . .

In October I went hunting with a party of seven on the head of the south fork of the flat head   we had 20 head of horses and them that wasent hunting elk was hunting horses   we shure got in a wild country and we had all the meat we wanted and brought back four elk   one of the party said he knew you   Hes an old N-N man   Dude Locket is his name   I dident kill aney thing but I had a good time   we were out three weeks. when we started home the party got split   four of us started with sevon pack horses   the other three stayed back to hunt horses   when we striped the packs that night we found we had all the meat no salt no coffe lots of shuger a tent but no flour and no bedding and the wethe was cold but thair was lots of wood so we made a big fire and eat our meat like a Ingun salt less but non of us eat much

Con I slept under saddle blankets be fore but I never had aney as smelly and hairy as these were   the rest of the party ove took us next day about noon   from that on we lived in comfurt   I will tell you more about it when we meet . . .

best whishes to you all from Jack Chaley and Nancy
Your friend
C M Russell

Aug 28
1915

Friend Berners

I got your letter and am mighty sorry to here about John. but feeling sorry is poor medison for sick friends so Im going to do the next cheep thing write him a Jollyup letter

Old John like the animal above is in a dam dangiros place but the goat dont think so and if I can make my friend feel like the goat I belive hel come across the bad pas

You said in your letter you were lonesum   whats the matter with packing youre war bag and drifting to my camp   a robe is spred and the pipe lit for you always

with best whishes to you and all friends

Your friend
C M Russell

St. Louis Mo
No 10th 1903

Friend Trigg

I thought I would write an let you know Im still among the live ones

I have taken in the worlds fair grounds   it is verry grand but dont intrest me much   the animal gardens which is near thair is more to my liking   they have a verry good collection among them a cyote who licked my hand like he knew me I guess I brought the smell of the planes with me   I shure felt sorry for him poor deval a life sentence for nothing on earth but looks an general princepales. but you cant do nothing for a feller whos hol famely is out laws as far back as aney body knowes, eaven if he is a nabor of yours   If he could make hair bridles it would bee a hol lot easier but with nothing to do but think of home its Hell thats all

Im stopping with my Folks who live verry neare the place where I was raised and altho the country is much bilt up there is some of the old land marks left an a little patches of woods enough to take me back to boyhood days and I was much suprised the other morning to scare up about 10 quail but as there is no shooting allowed that accounts for it   seeing these birds in this woods reminds me of when I was a youngster of about 9 winters hunting with a party of kids   we had one gun this wepon was the old time muzzel loding musket   there was but one boy in the party long enough to lode her with out the ade of a stump or log so of corse he packed the amuninition an don most of the loding   we were shooting in turns at aney thing in sight   well I kept belly aking saying My turn an the big kid saying Youl get yours an I did. When he loded for me I remember how the rod jumped clear of the barel   he spent five or more minutes tamping the loade then handing the gun to me said thair

a stump or log so of corse he packed the amunition an don nost of the loding we were shooting in turns at every thing in sight well I kept belly aking saying my turn an the big kid saying you l get yours an I did

when he looked for me I remember how the rod jumped clear of the barel he spent five minutes or more tamping the loade

then handing the gun to me said thair That would kill a tiger an I think it would if hed been on the same end I was

that would kill a tiger an I think it would if hed been on the same end I was My game was crows I climbed to the top of a rail fence to get cleane range. and then as the Books say for an instant my hawk eye mesured the glistening barrel then the death like stillness was broken by the crack of my fathfull wepon an I kept it broken with howls for quite a while. . . .

Your Friend
C M Russell

Hell o Trigg I'm here
in the big Camp
an have visited all the places that
interest me. an am getting lonsum
for home
I was down to the aquarium
the other day they have quite
a number of new fish
I walked back through Bowling
Green which I belive is the oldest
part of the burg
this is where the Dutch uste to
play ten pins

Hello Trigg

Im here in the big camp an have visited all the places that interest me. an am getting lonsum for home

I was down to the aquarium the other day   they have quite a number of new fish   I walked back through Bowling Green which I belive is the oldest part of the burg

this is where the Dutch uste to play ten pins an trade with the Indians. I think it was these limburger eaters that told the red man to plant powder an ball

Mr Ingen put in this crop the sam as corn.

but not beeing a up to date scientific dry lander his crop failed. the dutch like all good boosteres looked sorry an told him he hadent harrowed it under properly that by plowing deep an roling the soil would hold moister that it never had. the same as it did for our farmers last summer. did this stop the red man this plum failure of powder an ball crop   No   he started raising Hair without errigation   this crop was shurer but had its draw backs   imagin a savig who lived in the sweet smeling woods rasing the hair of a dutch man with limburger in every pocket   it must have been tough. right here Trigg I get hazy on history of this Iland but the Injun quit it and the English got it away from the Dutch. I dont know who owns it now but as every other man looks like Mose Kaufmans cousin I think Jerusilam has a large interist here

We took in a Suffereggte meeting the other night an a finer
band of Hell raisers I never saw bunched   according to there argu-
mant men would have littel to say in regards to goverment   I will
tell you all a bout it when I see you but will
close for this time, with regards to all

    Your friend
    C M Russell
   April 10
   1911

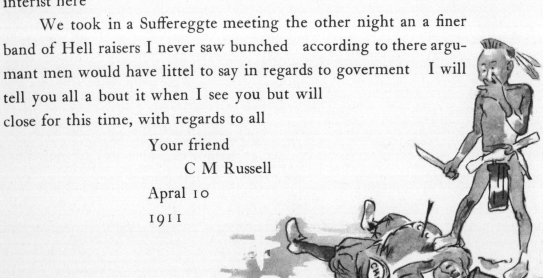

C. M. RUSSELL
GREAT FALLS, MONTANA

Pasadena Cal April 14 1920

Friend Bob the distence bared us from your

Friend Bob

the distence bared us from your Golden Wedding but thair is no trail to rough ore long to stop the travel of the good whishes of our harts to friends so our harts were with you at the scool house. Bob like all your friends we are glad we knew you. Your kind were never plenty. but thair scarce these days. Invention has made it easy for man kind but it has made him no better. Michinary has no branes A lady with manicured fingers can drive an automobile with out maring her polished nailes But to sit behind six range bred horses with both hands full of ribbons   these are God made animals and have branes. To drive these over a mountain rode takes both hands feet and head an its no ladys job   To sit on the nie wheeler with from ten to sixteen on a jirk line ore swing a whip ove twenty bulles strung on a chane an keep them all up in the yoke took a real man   And men who went in small partys or alone in to a wild country that swarmed with painted hair hunters with a horse under tham and a rifel as thair pasporte   These were the kind of men that brought the spotted cattel to the west before the humped backed cows were gon   Most of these people live now only in the pages of history. but they were regular men Bob and you were one of them   Some of them had wives mad of the same stuff as thair hus-bands true unselfish wimen and mothers who shared equely all hardships of the man of thair choise and desurved realy more prase than thair husbands   Bob you must have looked good to Miss Bickett for her to tie on to a cow trailing drifter like you Girls were scarce them days and Im betting thair were plenty of horses tied to old Doc Bicketts hich rack whos riders clamed to be looking for horses but were realy wife hunting. . . .

your friend

C M Russell

Friend Bill

I guess its about time I said some thing   the portrait was shure skookum an I was plenty supprised when Mame led me to it Christmas morning   you don yourself proud   I think its your best   You certainly spred paint while I was away

we got the spoon an the book of animal and bird beasts   the last will help me in my animal work

well Bill you may not belive it but I miss you   its kind of like missing the ache after the tooth is pulled   I often turn around from my work to cuss you an find nothing but the space where Duck leg sat

Percy an I with our good halves have just returned from Lewis Town where we met maney old timers some I hadent seen for over twenty years   we camped with Johny Ritch   neather He Percy nor I touched the goblet of joy   there was a stag banquet pulled of for us an some of the feeders got pie eyed not maple pied eather   it was a straight case of booze blinde   they couldent eaven see the New Year when it came in   I whish youd been with us   Id herded your hat. . . .

the sketch shows Duck leg hunting white tail in the Mission range   Linderman says your quetest man in the woods hes ever known   if the Kootenais who are great hunters had seen you they would have named you panther foot gost of the woods or som such titel . . . with best whishes from us both to yourself and Julie

Your friend

C M Russell

Aug 11
1918

Mr and Mrs John Lewis
Dear Friends

I left with out thanking you for the good time you gave me and my best half the above sketch will show that I dident sleep all the time I was at your camp these folks aint so fancy as the old time Injun nor as wild as the cow puncher but for variety of anatomy they got Injuns and cow folks skined to the dew claws.

I cant back track Howard further than the bufalo range on the Little Missouri but if hes Uncle to all them nephews and neices I met at your camp some of his brothers must have been Bisnops in Utah not buffalo hunters.

with meny thanks from us both

Your friend
C M Russell

Dont forget you are coming to our camp
and bring the three Bolingers

Jan 28 1916

Friend Guy

I received your letters an am a little slow about coming back with paper talk. But here goes I am glad to here you are going to pull another contest for the folks Those prizes your hanging up shure look good. But judging from horses and steers you delt out at Calgary and Winnipeg the rider or roper that takes a prize shure has something coming   I have lived among riders most of my life and late years Iv been taking in contests at different places but yours has got them all skined to the dew claws   An Il take my hat off to aney rider who takes or tryes to drag a prize from you   An Injun once told me that bravery came from the hart not the head. If my red brother is right Bronk riders and bull dogers are all hart above the wast band but its a good bet theres nothing under there hat but hair

well Guy I hope you git a cross all right and show them Cliff dwelers the real thing   they have all seen wild west shows but yours is no show its a contest where horses and ridirs are strangers   its easy when a bronk twister knows every jump in a hoss but hes gambling when he steps across one he never saw before   you savy

well guy I close with best regards to your self and Wife   Your friend

C M Russell

give my regards to Borine and all friends   we will be in New York about the first of March   then if you are still in the big camp we talk it over   is Ed Borine still in that owels nest on 42

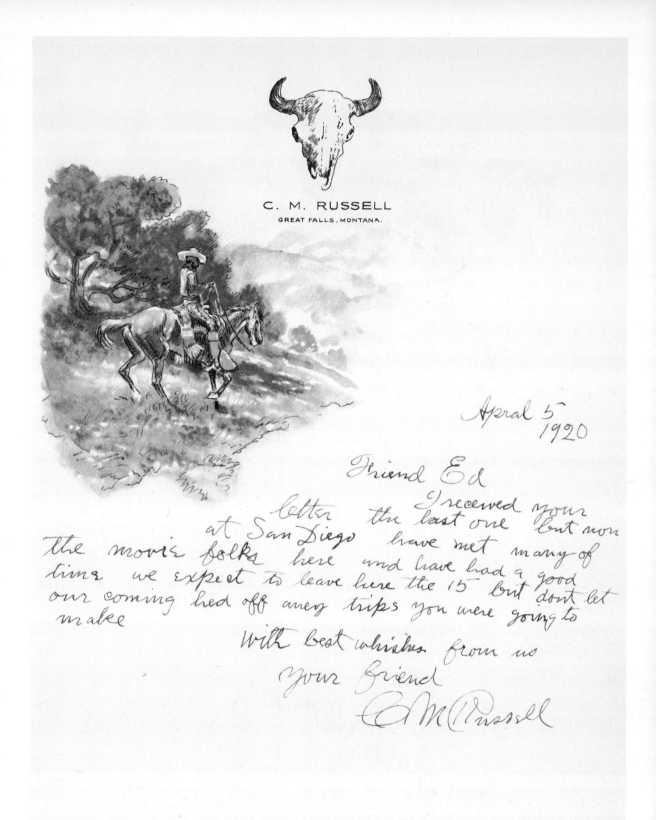

C. M. RUSSELL

GREAT FALLS, MONTANA.

Apral 5
1920

Friend Ed
I received your
letter the last one but non
at San Diego have met many of
the movie folks here and have had a good
time we expect to leave here the 15 but dont let
our coming hed off aney trips you were going to
make

With best whishes from us
Your friend
C M Russell

138

C. M. RUSSELL
GREAT FALLS, MONTANA

Frank Brown   *April 4* 1922

Friend Frank

I received your letter and was glad to here from you   their is not much to
write about down here so Il make my letter mostly picture   The sketch will show
you some of the folks that pass my camp   this kind ride the beaches of Calif   Its
hard to size up folks in this country but Im betting the he in the lead can get an
ace of the bottom   hes probably an oil man from Wyoming or a high class
burgelar from New York. The shes are wife and daughter of a well to do Boot leger
from Kansas   coming from that state of corse Maws strong for dry baring what she
uses around the house and the size drink she takes would make Bill Rance grinde
his teeth   both the henna haired daughter and her maw smoke privetly in Kansas but
wide open in Cal   Maw aint riding caus she loves horses but her Dock told her
it would remove leaf lard. the man in the drag cant be classed among the idle rich
he can count his coin with out taking it out of his pocket   Socially he aint got much
to say   him nor the hoss under him dont savy much but Spanish. their boath native
sons   Pedro maby thats his name dont know his fambly tree but its a safe bet his
mother was a pyute and his dad maby a Spanish Gentelman who gathered his coin
from the rode in the old stage coach day but compared to the hold up gents here to
day Pedros dad was in the kinder garden class   but this party would be out of luck
with out Pedro   hes like a packer with a pack trane, puts them on and takes them
off   if a pack slips hes their to set it up and see that it stays . . .

Your friend

C M Russell

139

Al Malison
killed by a falling horse
while cutting out on the beef
round up on the Mirias
range

Hon Paris. Gibson
Washington
DC

c/o Cochrane Hotel

6816 Odin st
Hollywood
Califonia

C. M. RUSSELL
GREAT FALLS, MONTANA

George Calvert

Friend Georg once more
were down with the jazz and geranuns
If its true that the Charlstown is hard on
buildings this country had better slow up
on that dance ore thair wont be a hous in it
that will stand a real shake an you know
they get som down here with out music
to play safe a rubber tent would be the shurest
but George you cant bluff a good sport and most of the folks here
that kind win ore loose they dont whine
here in Hollywood most of our nabers are moovie people
like the rest of the world they are good and bad the
ones I know are good
The fur baring animal in the sketch below is not
a bom thrower from Russia hes holding down a
job at some of the studioes maby he aint a good
actor but hes got the whiskers and all thats requred of him
is to know a littel more than the three horses he
drives in a Russian slay before the camra
hers one place where you can hold a job on your
looks if your cock eyed enough you can get a job 
George the last time I saw you you said maby
youd com to Calif we all wish you would
and go back with us in the car
Mane has a new Lincoln we expect to
start home early in June let us know
if you deside to come
with best regards to all your fambly
from us all. Your friend,
C M Russell.

141

As I imagine San Pedro
in 1820

C. M. RUSSELL

GREAT FALLS, MONTANA

Pasadena Cal

April 10
1920

Friend Phil I got your
letter and Sketch so long ago I m al most a shamed to answer it
but I was glad to here from you eaven if I am slow about saying so
you will see I m down among the roses this is a beautiful country all
right but its strictly man made I think in early days it was
a picture country before the boosters made real estate out of it but I m
about 100 years late the live oak is a native of this country and good
to look at but it dident looke warm enough so the land boomer stuck
in palm trees and plenty of roses this is bout so when the northern
traveler looks out of the steam heated Pulman and sees all these palms
and flowers he thinks hes in the tropicks when the trane stops he
unlodes and prepares to camp if its a warm day he dont lite the ground
toll sombodys sells him what he thinks is an oring grove but when it
develps its lemons this is the birth place of Bunko and bungiloos
Phil if I was painting frute flowers automobiks are flying mashines this
would be a good country but nature aint lived here for a long time
and thats the old lady I m looking for
Phil its mighty near time you mad another trip west I think about
the middle of July youd bitter load your war bag and drift to Belton
my shack will be open for you Lake McDonald is not what she ust to
be but thair are still some wild skots near the deer are quite tame and
we see them often if you com we l take another trunk line trip
think this over Phil

with best whishes to you and your Mother
from us all Your friend

C M Russell

we leave for home
next week

142

The Evolution of the Range Beef

Buffalo
1743 to 1832

Range Beef 1743 to 1832

Long Horn
1832 to 1875

Range Beef 1832 to 1875

White Face
1875 to 1925

Range Beef 1875 to 1925

One of Peblos riders

Friend Goodwin

I guess you think its about time I answred your last letter but you know me

if the moos you shot was like your sketch he was a dandy   I was out on a buffalo roundup in October   I wish youd been along   it was on the Flat Head reservation, an open, wild country   we saw lots of wild hosses never getting closer than a mile an dont ever think they wasent wild   it seemeded like they all ways winded us before we sighted them   they were all ways running   our camp was on the Pandrall river surounded by a high roling country   I was camped with the Canadin Officals who bought the buffilo 800 head owned by a Half Breed Peblo by name knowing the resivertion would bee throne open he asked Unkle Sam to leave him a range but Unkle wanted it for farmers   then he asked him to by them and when Unkel shook his head, the Canadians jumped in an grabed them at $250 a head   since the sale U S has made a buffilo pasture not 30 miles from Peblos range an our country has 4 head two of them presented by Conrad the other two by some man at Salt Lake a large heard for a country like ours   if it had not been for this animal the west woud have been the land of starvation for over a hundred years   he fed an made beds for our frounteer an it shure looks like we could feed an protect a fiew hundred of them but it seemes there aint maney thinks lik us

I am sending you a rough map of the trap that was bilt to cach the Buffilo

Peblos riders wer all breeds an fool bloods making a good looking bunch   The first day they got 300 in the whings but they broke back an all the riders on earth couldent hold them   they onely got in with about 120

I wish you could have seen them take the river   they hit the water on a ded run   that river was a tapyoker for them an they left her at the same gate   they tuck

144

her catching a phatographer from Butt City on the bank   we all thought he was a goner but whin the dust cleared he showed up shy a camra hat an most of his pants lucky for him there was som seeders on the bank an he wasent slow about using one

we all went to bed that night sadisfide with a 120 in the trap but woke up with one cow   the rest had climed the cliff an got away

the next day they onely got 6 an a snow storm struck us an the roundup was called off till next summer   if you come out this sumer we will go over an see it we can take the boat from Kalispell an go down the lake   its onely about 25 miles from the foot of Flat head lake to the trap an we could get horses thair an ride over.

I como back by the lake to Kalispell   it is a fine trip   Bob Benn sent his best whishes   he sent us some fine buffilo meet for Christmas

were are having a cold snap out here   last night it was 38 below o an it has been snowing for for days

give my regards to Dunten an all who know me

Whishing you and yours a happy New Year

Your friend

C M Russell

145

July 9 1926[1]

Friend Charles:

I got your letter and was glad to get it   we could use a lot of Neihart air here right now and I wouldent mind having a chunk of snow from Old Baldy and lay on a bow bed built by Bill Frip an Bill aint such a good bed builder but since I came to Rochester, I love aneything in Montana   if I had a ratler snake here and I knew he was from Arrowcreek I couldent keep my hands off him.

Well Charles tomorrow is Satterday and a week ago tommorrow I climed on the block and maby others dident know but it took every grane of sand I had   I tuck a local anasethic—local means nearby and it was so near by I dident miss much the feeling wasent bad but my eres were tuned up till I could here a bug whisper and the nois of the knife was plane   these Expurts were through in fifteen minutes but thats nothing—give one of these trimmers a good knife and hed skin and quarter Marcus Anderson in ten and wouldent nick his blade

Well Charles these fiew words will tell you that Im still this side of the Big Range—If nothing happens we expect to start home in ten days.

With best regards to you and yours

Your friend
C M Russell

[1]Written from the Mayo Brothers' hospital, Rochester, Minnesota, shortly before his death.

C. M. RUSSELL
GREAT FALLS, MONTANA

April 24 1923

Jim Bollinger

Well Judge I said I'd write
later an I guess this is late enough
were boath a long ways from the South fork but we
wont forget it we might forget Citys but hungary hoss
hoss heven soup creek pendigon spotted Bear and other
far off places where young men and old boyse shake hands
with misery and plesure we know both these ladys
and wont forget them Saw Mr. Mrs Foster than
looking good both sent regards to you met a lady
friend of yours a Miss Preston she told us Steave was
down at La Hoya Jim Hobbens is making up a party
to hunt Elk in Jacksons Hole next fall you are invited
I think its a good country Frank Linderman and fambly
ave been here all winter left a few days ago we leave
for home May first we all send regards to you all
                              Your friend
My regards to the Preohontas Club   C M Russell

147

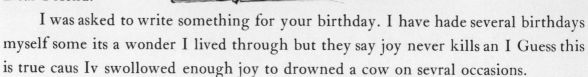

June 29 1916

Mr Paris Gibson,
Dear Friend:

I was asked to write something for your birthday. I have hade several birthdays myself some its a wonder I lived through but they say joy never kills an I Guess this is true caus Iv swollowed enough joy to drowned a cow on sevral occasions.

last year you wrote congratulating me on my success, but spoke as if you were afraid I might get swelled in the head and be near sighted when I passed friends. there is no danger of that, my Friend—talent like birth marks are gifts an no credit nor fault of those who ware them. It is onely men like you can clame credit.

In 1883 I night hearded horses where this town stands. I saw lots of grass plenty of water for the herds a good ford below Sun river. They were old men among us that spoke of it as a good beef county but there was nothing said of a town.

This country was dotted with buffalo skulls which brought to my Imagination many wild pictures but there were no citys among them.

Cow men said the falls were a drawback, they drowned lots of cattle an stoped boat travle.

But there was a man from New England a country where they rais more rock to the acer than aney other land under the sun an thats with out furtelizer ore erigation. This man did not paint pictures ore punch cows but his eyes saw a great city where there was only pararrie and rivers. He showed the people where the town would be: many of them laughed but he called the turn.

You my Friend was the camp finder and have all rights to be proud.

Our trails have not been the same but Iv often seen your tracks but never once have they back tracked ore taken water to fool their followers.

A birthday is onely a place on the trail of life where the travler stops to look back. Like the rest of us, you have rode some lame horses but the trail behind you will never be grass grone ore forggotten.

Your friend
C M Russell

148

Mr Andrew Pinker
Dear Friend Me an my friends
wish to thank you for the boost

wishing you luck in 1910 an the same right along till the
Chash in

GREAT FALLS, MONTANA.

TAKE THIS TO THE BUTTE OF MANY SMOKES

Chas Schatzlein
Butte Mont

C. M. RUSSELL
GREAT FALLS, MONTANA

Feb 26/1920

Friend Jim

aney time you ore any of your He ore She friends start thinking your loosing the beauty lines that youth gave you come to long beach and youl feel better nobodys bared Clothing is mad to hide ore lye but bathing suits are truthfull

for sevral years old dad time has been handing me things I dident want an I aint been thankfull for his favors but since I took a look at Long beach I think the Old Gents been Dam good to me we are camped now in a bunglow at Pasadena among flowers and palm trees that have been here long enough not to mind the cold ore maby the flowers are like the native sons they wont admit it A Califonia real estate man can stand mor cold with out humping his back than aney humans I ever knew its warem enough when the sun shines but when the sky wares scatering clouds and the sun plays peek a boo its like having chills and feaver . . .

your friend

C M Russell

866 Chestor av north Pasadena, Cal

150

Missoure Jim is married and has

a ranch on peoples creek
his nearest nabor is man that sets high
he calls on Jim quite often sets high dos
not belong to the working class
but it can never be said that he
will not help with a workin man
because he often comes over at
noon time and helps Jim eat

Jan '6 1919

Dear Judge

  Im a fiew moons late coming across with thanks
   for the invitation you sent me to join in the big hunt
an you got plenty of reasons to think I'm a piker so I'm sending in this ink talk to
squar myself its going to be hard work caus Im mighty lame with a pen. . . .

  In the first place long before you and Lewis talked of your hunt I had promised
my friend Frank Linderman a visit at his camp on Flat Head Lake but I had called
that off and was going to throw in with the Bollinger and Lewis bunch then the
flew broke out and throws a scare in me and this old sickness surtenly trimed this
camp heres prufe enough I just sold a picture to an undertaker

  So as long as old flew rode heard on my camp I dident care to take a long
chance if I went with you to the south fork Id be out of reach of letter or wire so
I played safe and went to Lindermans his camp is right on the road I stayed with
Frank about ten days done som fishing and had good luck onley hunted three
days saw lots of sign Frank got one white tail thairs plenty of deer round his
camp but thair shure man wise I hope you all had good luck I would like to eat
som elk stake that you cooked . . . My Wife Jack and I whish you all a Happy
New Year

          Your friend
          C M Russell

MERRY ENGLAND

MAY 14
1914

Senitor Paris Gibson

Dear Friend

Here we are in the midle of the Atlantic a bord the Lusitania. Lusitania I think meanes Hold up judging from the easy way the owners take money

The boat I went over in was a hotel   this one is a town about the size of Lewistown an its no slur on that camp eather

we are a littel north of the trail that Columbus broke   our boat aint as safe but wer going faster but Cris wasent in no hurry   he was onley looking for America . . .

I have seen quite a little of old England an its sertenly a pritty country like one great park with an interesting history   I viseted seviral hang outs of Bill the Conquar   saw walls and rodes built before Bill landed by the Romans. saw the ax and block where maney politicans lost there office. an when I looked at that old rustay ax I couldent help thinking that it might be a good thing these days   It sertanly has made a clean quiet country of England a land which for centuries lay seeped in blood   the history of our country has quite a littel read in it but its pale compared to this land   our Injun was a ware lover but blamed no God for the blood he spilt   neather for Cross or King did he war but for his country an well we know it was worth fighting for a Dam good country an a Dam good cause   the Injun was bad all right but Senitor if time were to slip her cogs an drop back some senturies Id prefur scary America to Merry England . . .

With best whishes to you and most of the folks in Montana

Your friend

C M Russell

153

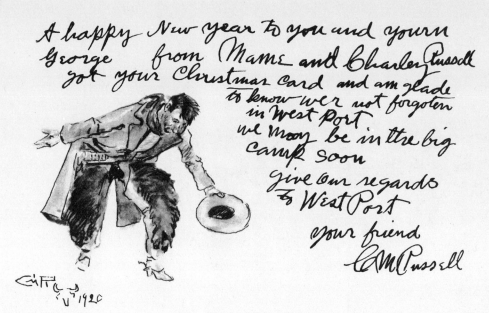

A happy New year to you and yourn
George   from Mame and Charley Russell
got your Christmas card and am glade
to know wer not forgoten
in West Port
we may be in the big
camp soon
give our regards
to West Port
your friend
C M Russell

(Card to George Wright, artist.)

Howard Eaton
Wolf
Wyoming

Friend Young Boy I
received the shield and
pictures they wer all fine
and I thank you verry
much I will paint
your picture as soon
as I can

Your Friend
C M Russell

Frank B. Brown
Friend Frank

Address R 3 Box 223
Pasadena Calafonia
May 4 1924

    I got your letter and was glad to here from you but dont think I could build up on that custerd pie diat you advise   I cant forget that littel talk you gave me on custard   Frank the above sketch aint a hold up   its what the hoof and mouth disease has don to the beautiful rodes in Califonia   the quarintene gard has stoped a car   the law says no animal ore vegitable frute ore flower that grows above ground can pass   The dogs out of luck if his friends don't return   fido don't bark no more at the moon   Hes as good as weiners right now

    The lady to the right aint going to be hung ore have a hair cut   Shes been picking popyes and was caught with the goods so thair going to fumigate her and when thair through she couldent stay at a skunk bording house but she could live a month in a leper camp and leave with out a pimple . . . You will notice the ladys in my sketch are scared but dont turn pale   they cant   the wimen to day have got nature cheeted   a lady that can blush ore turn pale through her make up had better see a doctor   shes got blood preshure . . .

    Califonia is all right but I can't see belt ore squar butte from here   Frank give my best whishes to Montana   nobodys bared

Your friend
C M Russell

March 24
1926

Dear Miss Josephine

I want to thank you for the nice birth day card you sent and your Shamrock has brought luck as I feel much better to day   not that Iv been sick but I havent felt real good   That card was shure a Paddys greeting   maby Im not Irish but my fondness for that Race makes me belive Im a breed. . . .

Miss Josephine Califonia is not the country that Bret Hart knew but the moovie people still make romance   The English woods you see on the screen at the Liberty or aney other show house are realy live Oaks in Cal

So you see in 1926 when everything is forgoten but right now you are apt to meet armored men of Ritchard the Lion Harteds time

A fiew years ago, you might of seen Moses and his bunch heading for the Sea somwhere betwine Long beach and Santa Barbra   maby they had harps but if they played it was jass music the same as youl here at the Odan ore Meadow Lark Club.

Moses is here yet   I saw him the other day   I don't know what he's doing now but its a safe bet he cant write the Ten Commadments. . . .

With best whishes to yourself and Mother and Miss Furnald from us all

Your friend

C M Russell

March 10
1920

Charles F Lummis

I have eaten and smoked in your camp and as our wild brothers would. I call you Friend   Time onley changes the out side of things. it scars the rock and snarles the tree but the heart inside is the same   In your youth you loved wild things   Time has taken them and given you much you dont want. Your body is here in a highley civilized land but your heart lives on the back trails that are grass grown ore plowed under   If the cogs of time would slip back seventy winters you wouldent be long shedding to a brich clout and moccasens and insted of beeing holed up in a man made valley youd be trailing with a band of Navajoes headed for the buffalo range

I heap savy you caus thaird be another white Injun among the Black feet Hunting hump backed cows

My brother when you come to my lodge the robe will be spred and the pipe lit for you   I have said it

Your friend
C M Russell

158

1910

Friend Con

I guess you will be supprised to here from me but I thought I would let you know how we are getting along

I just got back from a visit with John Matheson   he sold his teem an bought bench land ranch about 20 miles from here   the above sketch showes what it looks like   it was cold an plenty of snow   the pump froze up   we decided to take it out so both o us started liftin   thairs a sheet o ice and we cant no moren keep our feet we got her pritty near the top   John sliped   the pump handel hit me on the head and the spout caut John back of the year   when he got to his feet he made a run for the ax an the talk he used wouldent look good in print   it was shure strong but it dident get the pump out   neather did we. an John gets his water hand over hand   it onely takes 3 or 4 ours to water a horse but that all goes with the independent life of the farmer

well Con we had a pritty good Christmas an we thought an talked of you all an we would have liked to have you here. . . . I hope you are all getting along fine   Id lik to be up there and help Mrs P bild another calf shed . . .

we both send best whishes to your self Wife and Lesley

Your friend

C M R

159

September 26
1926

Dr Philip Cole
                    Friend Cole
I just received your gift the books by
Will James
which I like verrey much
when it comes to horses nobody can beat
James
thair is no other horse like our range
horse and James savys every moove they make
we have just returned from our mountian
camp
the big hills look verry beautiful in
thair fall clothing of maney colers
the above sketch is of a small band of
Elk we saw a few days before we left
which I hope will remind you of the
country you were born and raised in
the camp you live in now can bost
of man made things
but your old home is still the real
out doors

and when it coms to making the beautiful
Ma nature has man beat all ways from
the ace
and that Old lady still owns a lot of
montana
to show what I mean man made this
animal   but the old lady Im
takina   about made this one

                    I have made a living painting
                    ofpictures of the horned ox and
the life about him it took regular men
to handle real cows
I would starve to death painting the hornles
deformity
God made cows with horns to defend herself
and when a wolf got meat it wasent easy
often he was so full of horn holes he wasent
hungry
a weasel could kill the man one with out
getting a serach
but I forgot Iv got no kick coming Iv
been turned my self
but the medicine men at Rochester
onely took from me things I dident need
and was glad to get rid of
I look and feel better but Im still very
weak
if you see Olaf Seltzer give him my
regards
I suppose by this time hes a real Newyorker
we have been having lots of snow but today
it has cleard and I think the storm is over
we all send our best regards to you and
yours   your friend
                    C M Russell